MW00425361

"In this luminous memoir Shuly Cawood dives into the deepest of waters—health and illness, the bonds of family, intimacy and its unraveling—and emerges with a treasure. The writing is beautiful, both spare and lush, and the wisdom to be discovered there is genuine and hard won. *The Going and Goodbye* is a revelation."

— Matthew Goodman, *New York Times* bestselling author of *Eighty Days* and *The Sun and the Moon*

"These true stories about love and loss will recalibrate your heart. There are scenes and characters and brilliant details of a life, as there are in other fine memoirs, but there's something here besides. Something rare. There's language that surprises and stuns, that forces you to catch your breath again and again and holds the very rhythm of sensation. You quickly realize that you can't glance from a single page (from a single line) without risking the loss of some subtle insight about love—all sorts of love—that helps you understand your own humanity. This is a brave writer who moves lyrically and fearlessly toward self-knowledge, a writer who is willing to probe the darkness in the chambers of her own heart, not just the hearts of others. Hope in this book is realistic and hard-won. No false note strays onto the page. This is a voice you can trust with your life."

— Joyce Dyer, author of *Gum-Dipped* and *Goosetown*

"This memoir ranges all over the past while creating a steady sense of forward motion through the narrator's life. I think of these two streams of energy as lyric and narrative, the circling and moving forward. The two have a great dynamic here, which keeps this memoir surprising and fresh."

— Kathryn Rhett, author of *Souvenir* and *Immortal Village*

"In this lovely memoir the narrator, although strongly rooted in a particular place, is always on the move into the unknown. But she's trying to find her way home, through a landscape of love and loss. The lyrical, fluid style immediately invites the reader along for the ride. I read this with great pleasure!"

— Bobbie Ann Mason, PEN/Hemingway Award winning author of *In Country* and *The Girl in the Blue Beret*

the

GOING

and

GOODBYE

a memoir

SHULY XÓCHITL CAWOOD

PLATYPUS PRESS, England

Copyright 2017 by Shuly Xóchitl Cawood
All rights reserved.

Excerpt from "The Writer," from *Collected Poems
1943–2004*, by Richard Wilbur. Copyright 2004
by Richard Wilbur. Reprinted by permission of
Houghton Mifflin Harcourt Publishing Company.

This book is a recollection, though
some names have been changed for privacy.

ISBN 978-0-9935321-9-1

First Edition, 2017

Cover and interior layout by Peter Barnfather
Type set in Bergamo Pro, FontSite Inc.

Published by Platypus Press

for Preston, always

It is always a matter, my darling,
Of life or death, as I had forgotten. I wish
What I wished you before, but harder.

Richard Wilbur, "The Writer"

THE GOING AND GOODBYE

Young Love

We dug for pesos in our pockets. The coins were round and shiny and heavy. Without a word, the man took the money from our outstretched hands.

Rob had pale skin, like winter, thick eyebrows and green eyes the shade of a sea I had only seen in pictures. I had long dark hair and slender fingers that might have played piano well but did not, and a dimple that only appeared when I smiled. We were both twenty-eight and had known each other for five months. Days before that amusement park ride, we had decided to spend our lives together.

I was the one who had seen the ride and wanted to try it. I thought I knew exactly what it would be like. I often thought that then—that I could guess the future and be right. Now I look back on that day—and so many others before and after—and wonder at all the things I missed.

The ride spun two ways: First, it threw its mechanical being into a circular motion, with arms like spokes on which buckets hung, orbiting the center. And second, one's own bucket—ensconcing two people in a spinning world—would also spin itself, twirling passengers as if they were caught in a pinwheel. One could tug at the round, metal plate at the bucket's center and make everything spin faster. I put Rob in charge of that. He had more muscle, I reasoned, and would not mind.

I remembered rides of my youth when my father sat between me and my sister and tugged at the same kind of metal plate, tugged so that we could only see the blur of the world. We squealed, begging him to pull harder, and he always did.

Rob had acquiesced to the ride, though later I would wonder whether he ever wanted on in the first place. That's what love does: makes you promise things you want to yank back later.

The man charged with the ride had a face that seemed tired of containing emotions. It was flat and somber and silent. After taking our money, he ambled to a bucket, lifted its metal rod of an arm, let us in, and shoved the bar back into place. It clicked, like a gun, the sound of both a beginning and an end.

There was no one else on the ride.

It was a warm late July afternoon in Acapulco. We had gone to Mexico to be in love, to venture into the unknown future. Between us we knew enough Spanish to order simple food—tacos with *pollo*, or *enchiladas* with *salsa verde*—and we could manage to ask for one hotel night or three or four, and if we fumbled for words or the right tense of a verb, we could laugh about it later. This language had served us from Oaxaca to Huatulco to Puerto Escondido and now in Acapulco. We had eaten *paletas* every day, popsicles of creamy coconut and juicy mango, and we had slept well and slept in and stolen AC for two hours in the cinema. We juggled guidebooks and pulled out maps and folded them back up along lines not quite clear but close enough. We heaved a striped, woven blanket onto buses and then back off again, a blanket that was really too heavy to carry, to haul along with us. But we did not think twice about it. We kept on heaving, sure we had what we needed and would always need.

And now, on this desultory afternoon, we waited for the man as he ambled to his booth as if he had done this a thousand times and could not possibly bear it once more.

But then he cranked the ride going, and it lurched into motion, and up, up we rose, our bucket lifting toward the heavens and down, down to earth, and up, up again so that, though the bucket spun, we glimpsed the rest of the amusement park, a temporary collection of rides that jangled and clanked, and of people who up and moved wherever the rides went, who served fried foods and cold candy and drinks perspiring in cans and cups, and who showed off plastic toys you could win if you knew how to throw, or had luck, which as we rose in our bucket, we might have guessed, if someone had asked, we had plenty of, not knowing luck was a scent—like buttered popcorn or caramel apple— that drifted in the other direction with one capricious gust.

The man charged with the ride—a man I would conjure up later with dark, slicked back hair and droopy eyelids—began to throttle our small bucket, and it occurred to me then that only he could say how long, how much, and that the spinning, which was now quickening, would end only if the man allowed it.

The ride threw us up, up, and down, down, and our bucket spun so fast we slid into each other, smashed skin to skin, and the fair and everything we could see blurred and washed together in an uneasy glimpse, again, again, and neither one of us laughed as the pace quickened, as we spun so fast everything I had ever eaten tossed in my gut, and round and round we went until the sky was in our laps and our bodies felt as if we could not press harder against the bucket's edges, and up we tossed and down we came and up again and down and up and down and up and down until the dizziness felt like failure.

The ride slowed and stopped. The man ambled over. He lifted the metal rod and let us loose, and we staggered off the ride for which we had paid. We held our stomachs and could not bear the scent of sizzling meat, nor could we look at the fruit in market stalls, their peels broken and the flesh sweltering through. We could not have glanced at scarves swaying in the breeze nor born the sound of water beating against the shore.

We returned to our hotel room and lay on separate beds. We turned on our sides and on our backs, but nothing kept the world from free falling.

Outside, the sun dropped its yellow, heavy head. The last light then drained out of the sky.

CHAPTER ONE

The Summer of Uno

His name was Raúl. He was nineteen years old, slightly stocky, and had a warm, gravelly voice, a deep laugh. He had thick, dark hair and a face flecked with freckles. He smoked God-knows-how-many-packs of cigarettes. He was my cousin Víctor's good friend, and that summer, Raúl spent the hot desert afternoons playing Uno with me and my sister and Víctor on the floor of my *tía's* television room.

In Uno, the goal is to get rid of all of your cards; you get points from what everyone else has left in their hands. If you've never played the game, here's all you need to know: It's a game largely of luck and chance, a game in which you cannot tell when you might have to switch directions or skip a turn, or worse, draw cards you don't want. Sure, there are wild cards to discard when you have nothing else to play, but some carry penalties for other players—someone always pays the price for what you don't have.

I was thirteen and new to Uno, new to so much that summer.

I had flown with my family to Mexico to visit my mother's oldest sister, Estela, in Torreón, along with her husband—my Tío René— and their four children, two of whom had already married and moved into their own houses but still bustled in and out of my *tía's* house on Allende for chit-chat, a snack, Sunday lunches, and quick coffee breaks. The house had red tile floors, white stucco arches, and a courtyard with a fig tree. The room where we played Uno had a soft couch beneath windows that faced the city street. In between us and the world of beeping cars, exhaust fumes, and passing lanes, a black wrought-iron fence rose. At its gate, men came by to sell things —stacks of warm tortillas, bottles of cold *leche*—and through the gate, the maid came and went, my cousin Lalin's suitors came and went, and Raúl came and went, and I didn't know then that in other summers I would gaze out those windows and watch for his return, and that he never would again—except once, two years later, to catch a glimpse and say goodbye.

That summer, I did not yet know Spanish, but Raúl knew enough English to make up for what I lacked. That was the year I slimmed down, the year I cut bangs and grew my hair long, the year I cared about brand-name jeans, the year of my first kiss. Raúl liked me, but I was too young. Still, he was kind enough to take my cousins' teasing, to give me the silver ring they slipped to him beneath the table at Martin's diner, a thin band of silver—a ring I would later realize was not a circle of promises but of memories. He was kind enough to lean down and put his face to mine as I sat blindfolded at Víctor's party the night before I left for home. It was a game, and I was to guess who was leaning down, kissing my cheek, and I was young enough to believe I could guess right about who he was, who he might one day be. I guessed Raúl. I guessed I was in love.

I wrote him a letter or two when I got home, and it must have been months later that he wrote back. I only remember that by the time his letter arrived in my black mailbox, it was cold out, the days had shortened, and the light had leaned into a slant. My Ohio landscape told of fallow fields and skies grey with winter's breath. Raúl wrote to me on paper that was almost as translucent as water, and his words slipped across the pages. He confessed that he was studying to become a priest and had known that in the summer but not said so. He was telling me now that he was already *comprometido*: committed, promised, otherwise engaged.

I did not know it then, but it would not be the last time I would feel against God in the wish for someone's affection. It wouldn't be the last time my mother's native Mexico would become tangled with love and loss, that Torreón would be a place of swerving into newness and letting go. It wouldn't be the last time that words would startle, hurt, and shift me.

I was so young then. Perhaps it was better I did not know.

CHAPTER TWO

Gunning It

To understand love, you must first understand power—the balance of it, when to give it up, when to take it back. You must understand how to be responsible with it.

When I was sixteen, my father taught me to drive. One of his most important lessons: how to stop a stick-shift car from sliding back on a steep hill. The trick was releasing the emergency brake while pressing the gas pedal, so you took power from one thing and gave it to the other. But you had to be focused, and this switching had to happen in just a second.

In general, manual-transmission cars required more attention and precision, skills my father wanted me to have when at the steering wheel. Having to use both feet helped. Also, he did not want me to ever become stranded because I did not know how to work a stick shift, so one Saturday he taught me to drive in his Volkswagen Rabbit: he took me twenty miles from home to downtown Dayton, Ohio, to throttle back and forth along Ludlow and Jefferson and by the old Rikes department store, where my mother used to take me and my sister to shop and gaze at the Christmas window displays decked in gold and tinsel.

The day he taught me to drive, I stalled the little brown car all over Dayton. We staggered down the streets. We chugged around city blocks in his diesel-engine auto that had broken down every time we drove through Tennessee to see my father's aunt in Vicksburg, Mississippi.

But that day, the Rabbit did not fail me. That day, I learned to press pedals with my left and right foot in a rhythm that was almost a dance.

When I was seventeen, I borrowed my mother's beloved Honda Accord one afternoon. It was the first car that was really hers—not a shared family car, and not my father's. She even chose its color, a red like the belly of a ripe cactus tuna. I took the Accord so I could go and see a movie in Beavercreek, a town fifteen miles away, with my friend Jon. We were driving on Fairfield Road on our way home, the speed limit was no more than forty, forty-five, and thank goodness I was not zipping down the two-lane, but I know now I was driving too closely to the car in front of me because it stopped or at least slowed to a near-halt, and I turned away for a moment to look over at Jon while we chatted, and before I could look back, I smashed into the rear of the other car.

The other driver—I remember only that he was bearded and could have easily been my father's age—barreled out of his car, ranting as he moved toward me, stopping just outside my window. I could not move from my seat, could only say *I'm so sorry* and wince at the man's jabbing words. Finally, it was Jon— he must have been only fifteen or sixteen then—who yanked on his door handle, sprinted over to my side of the car, and stepped in front of the raised voice and gesturing arms and said *take it easy*. Jon's voice hung evenly in the air, a calm and steady line in contrast to my jittery hands, my heart shaking in my chest.

My mother would be grateful I was unharmed, but I shuddered at the car's crumpled hood, at knowing that in losing focus, I could wreck a thing so loved, so easily.

When I was twenty-six and twenty-seven, I lived in Oxford, Ohio, a small town that stilled outside my apartment window at night, trees frozen by late fall, black branches crooked as if searching for warmth. The walls of my apartment seemed thin like moth's wings against the cold.

I put in long, hard hours at a job I did not love. I refused to quit the position—even though I longed to—because I had an idea about the number of years I should stay at the job. Rules, propriety, and duty often overthrew the things I truly wanted.

My boss was a man who wore big, shiny cuff links and crisp shirts. One day, my co-worker pulled me into her office and said the boss did not think I was working hard enough.

"Why would he think that?" I asked.

"Because you leave at five every day," she said, even though she knew I lugged home paperwork and files to read every night. "If I were you," she said, "I'd work at the office past five—just stay until he leaves."

At the ends of days, even when the backs of my shoes cut into my ankles or my skirt pinched my waist, I remained stranded at my desk instead of standing up, instead of gunning out the door. At night, back at my apartment, I ate accompanied by silence or by the intermittent arguing of the couple across the hall. The fluorescent fixture between our doors twitched with light.

I was in the middle of a frantic dance of relationships back then, dizzily saying goodbye to a friend I loved—a man with soft, short hair, a former gymnast who unfolded emotions in long-distance letters and who had little confidence that he wanted to marry anyone, ever, much less me—and stumbling toward a man I worked with who had thick lips, a laugh that boomed like a drum, and hair with ends curled like fists. What did I know then of power and balance? He tucked a pencil behind his ear when stalking around the office, and he erased me when angry, his face turning blank during disagreements whenever I tried to talk, which I did, heedlessly, even when he asked me to stop.

I did not tell anyone how he could stonewall me for days.

One morning, I was hurrying toward work, pressing the gas pedal down South College Avenue, just blocks from my apartment. I was in my very first car, a baby-blue Honda Civic my parents had bought for me, taken out a loan to purchase, given me with a maintenance schedule my father drafted, which I followed to the mile.

That morning, in my haste, I did not see the car approaching me in the opposite lane. I swung left to turn and rammed into the left side of his front fender. Moments later, the driver emerged from his car into the glistening, shattered glass.

I was lucky, really, in my carelessness, that I only got a ticket, a court date, pangs of guilt, and that the other driver had not broken an arm or leg, or died—that I had not. I could simply go on if I chose to. If I chose well.

While in Oxford, I traveled for work in a company sedan—a bulky Ford Taurus the color of dark blood. One morning, the air foggy and heavy and damp, the sun not quite up, I was somewhere in northern Ohio near an empty train track, stopped at a red light, behind another car. The man in front started to turn right, so I released my brake, pressed the gas, and then he stopped again, and in that moment—that I wanted to take back but was helpless to—I banged into his bumper. Yet another man I had risked running into out of carelessness. This time, just a fender bender, no injuries, no totals. We stood in the cold, hunched in our jackets, waiting for the police to arrive.

And then one late afternoon I was driving again in a company sedan but this time not in a city or town but on a flat country road, no steep hill that signaled *pay attention*. Fields unfurled on either side of the lane, and I let my attention lapse—looked in the glovebox? Changed the radio dial? I don't remember. All I know is I was heading toward Oxford again—the sunless apartment, the cufflinked boss, the sometimes sullen co-worker I had chosen to let into my life—and then I was sliding off the road, hitting berm and gravel and skidding, the car whorling until I slammed the brakes and stopped. The car had not flipped over, and no one had witnessed the spinning, whirring blur of me let loose upon the edges of unsown fields. No barn, no farmhouse in sight. Just me in the cold white of day, shutting the engine to silence.

What are you doing?

I lay my head back.

I waited for my breathing to slow down before I stepped out to check the car for gravel pocks and dings. I saw nothing but the thinnest, slightest scratch, as if someone had tried to scrawl something on the back fender, and then tired and given up.

What are you doing?

Later, I would tell no one what I had done. Although I trembled at that moment, I started the ignition and turned onto the empty road, driving toward Oxford and all the choices I had made and swearing to God I would be more careful, that I would never do this again.

CHAPTER THREE

The Stray

I was alone in the back seat when it happened. I remember city lights and cars hustling down lanes, and listening to the voices of my mother's sister and her husband, my *tíos*, who were in the front seat and speaking to each other in Spanish, a language I had finally come to understand.

There was a moment just before it happened when the world before me stilled and then stopped.

Torreón, Mexico, burned hot and dry, even at night, but I remember that evening in March as something else: wet, slippery, a place where you could wreck and ruin something if you weren't careful enough.

If you don't know where you are going, seek the needle of a

compass. It was my father who taught me how to use and trust one. A black compass has bobbed on the dashboard of every car he has ever owned, positioned exactly in the middle, right where he can see it.

When my parents got me my first car, my father bought me my own small compass, peeled off the adhesive backing, stuck it on the dashboard, and adjusted the declination to make sure the compass pointed true north. I became used to glancing at that compass when I felt lost or when I was trying to make my way to a place I had never been before. And when I moved to a new city, a new town, when the roads got blurred in my mind, I thought of positions: the post office is north of my place; the university is east of the grocery store.

But in Torreón, there was no compass in the car I drove—a borrowed car, which I rarely drove at that—so I had to rely on instinct and memory to get me anywhere, to signal me when I needed to turn around and go a different way.

At twenty-four, I had left Ohio for Torreón to teach English for a semester; to live with Tía Tela and Tío René in their white stucco house, by then fully emptied of their grown children; to finally immerse myself in and learn my mother's first language. But there had been another reason to go, one I did not voice but that I heard more clearly: I wanted to know who I was without Matthew, the man I had been seeing by then for seven months. I felt I was losing myself, and now, looking back, I think the only way I was capable then of differentiating myself from him was by running away. And that would have been fine had I simply run, but what I did instead was run and still hold on.

I was often in the back seat during the months I lived in Torreón: I was driven to stores, driven to cousins' houses, driven to work and then back again. I had gotten a Mexican license a few weeks into my stay, and though Tía Tela let me take the car when she did not need it, I heard stories of policemen stopping drivers for the most minor offenses, leaning with hot breath into their windows, pressing, in low tones, for bribes. I drove white-knuckled and with one foot jabbing at the brakes, so I didn't say no when my *tíos* offered to drive to the bus station to pick up Matthew, who had come to visit in March all the way from Ohio, taking bus after bus to reach me.

Matthew and I had started dating the summer before, that time of year when the sun in Ohio beats strong and high. It had felt, then, as if the heat would never relent. We had eaten vanilla cones, swum in chilled pools, and slept under the hum of an old AC unit. I knew after only a few months I wanted to marry him, follow him anywhere he cared to go. Instead, throughout the fall, as orange leaves slipped from branches in the rain, Matthew talked of moving to another city, by himself. "We'll keep dating," he promised. "I'll come back and visit you." He did not ask the question I wanted him to, so I devised a plan of my own to make me forget the things he did not say. I kept my plan a secret, as if the only way I could keep from losing myself completely was to hide things.

I told myself I trusted he would find a way to me, or I would circle back, but making plans without the one you love is a sideways sort of lie. By December, the days in Ohio had contracted, casting out light at their starts and ends. That was when, as we lay in my bed, I blurted it out: I was leaving the country in January, in a matter of weeks.

Matthew laughed, "Yeah, sure."

But when I did not laugh with him, he sat straight up. A shadow lingered on his face. "Really?"

"Yes," I said. It was the answer to the question he had never asked, and the word felt tired and tiny and somber.

His shoulders fell, and I looked away.

We slept that night, as we always did, so close we could steal each other's breath.

Matthew's trip to Torreón in March was meant to erase the separation, to mitigate the facts: that I was learning a language he did not know; that I had missed him more on the days when we had lived in the same city and he did not have time to see me than I did in Torreón; that although all along I had been the one ready to get engaged, in February, when Matthew had finally said by email, phone, *okay, yes, let's*, I'd whooped it up but then taken it back two days later, telling him I was no longer ready. The truth is I was suddenly frightened at the idea—I was starting to grasp that I'd rushed myself and him, that I'd been blinded by our initial fast and furious falling in love. I was angry, too, that he realized what he wanted only after I had left for Mexico. It did not occur to me that my leaving had been in some ways an act of extortion. All I knew was I was no longer sure of myself or what I wanted and that my figuring it out was becoming messy. My ambivalence cursed us both, but it cursed him more. I thought the visit would bring Matthew back, or bring me back, but to what or where I did not know.

That's what Mexico had done in two months. That's what eighteen hundred miles between two people can do. Or maybe that's just what people do when they are afraid and caught, not knowing which way to go: they struggle toward an undetermined and terrible middle.

My *tíos* drove me to the bus station to pick him up. I opened the glass doors, stepped inside, and scanned the row of orange bucket chairs fastened to the floor. I spotted Matthew before he saw me, and he seemed smaller than I remembered. Not that his body was big: he was around six feet tall but thin. (Once, I had pulled on his jeans, which he had discarded on the bedroom floor, and had to tug them up my own slender legs and to my waist. When I frowned at their tightness, he said, "They look way better on you," before putting an arm around my waist to draw me to him. "You're a woman. That's what they're supposed to look like.") But Matthew's perfect posture always increased his height, bulked his chest and shoulders. He had a pet peeve about people who slouched, so I straightened when around him. Yet at that bus station in Torreón, it was hard to imagine him with his booming voice, as the one making jokes and commanding attention in a room. I had fallen in love, in part, because of how big his spirit was, how small I could let mine be. But across the room, Matthew looked hunched, his wiry frame bunched into a chair. He clutched the duffel bag on his lap—a bag that in my memory now appears enormous, dwarfing him.

When I was younger, my parents' love was big to me. Their story allowed me the latitude to think I could fall in love swiftly, torrentially, and that it could all work out. I suppose I still believe that, only this belief is tempered with a history so different from theirs.

On their first date, my father took my mother to eat at a Chinese restaurant, to a foreign film, *The Servant*, and out dancing at Le Flame. He squeezed her hand once while they danced because he liked her so much, and my mother liked it but thought it a little forward. Afterward, they sat in his grey VW Bug and talked until the early hours. He didn't kiss her until it was time to say goodbye.

I'd like to think that after that night my father couldn't stop thinking about my mother, that it's why he called her up the next day and asked to drop by, why he says now it was like being pulled by a magnet, why they got engaged six months after they met, and why they married soon after. When I was young, I wanted to believe in destiny and fate, maybe because it was romantic and easier than believing—as I did later, after marriage—that love was a series of choices you made from one day to the next. Easier than thinking love might be latched to duty, respect, and difficulty, and that sometimes you had to hold on to a thing that hurt in order to outlast the pain.

Through the rubble of years, any specific memory of Matthew's visit to Torreón—back when I was twenty-four—comes to me in pieces, a shard of a moment here, a broken bit there, as if the whole is unimaginable in its betrayal of how close we had been but no longer were. I can see now that we were both fighting to reclaim what was rightfully ours: for Matthew, all the love I'd promised; for me, his shelter, and at the same time, my freedom.

During his visit, he constantly smiled, asked my relatives questions, rolled out the few Spanish expressions he knew, and sampled all the food set in front of him—*jocoque*, *chorizo*, fruit speckled with *chile*. Matthew even attempted one afternoon to converse with Tío René, who knew only a little English. I came down the hallway and from a distance saw them, sitting in metal chairs, elbows on kitchen table, both of them straining but determined to speak. I waited and listened as they bent toward each other and repeated phrases and searched for words in their differing languages—ones impossible to find since they were never in their vocabulary to begin with. After several rounds of grunts and gestures, they simultaneously laughed and leaned back. Isn't that what I had wanted when I invited the man I loved—for him to like them, for them to adore him? My throat clenched, and I looked down at the tiled hallway and let the quiet swell once more.

Before Matthew's visit, I had convinced myself I wanted to share every bit of my *tíos'* house with him: the arches and circular staircase; the balcony from which I could see people sweeping their sidewalk in the early hours of morning; and the smell of the house—oh, the smell—of warming and yeasty *bolillo*, of roasting chicken, of beans stewing with onions and peppers. But now that Matthew stood beside me, I held my breath. The rooms shrank when we sat alone, as he reached over for my hand. I held on and then withdrew, held on and then withdrew.

Before, he had led and I had followed, but that March we shifted into new positions. If we walked to the *alameda*, it was I who led us around the tree-lined block, through the clusters of families eating popsicles and *elotes*, and by the couples draped over each other on benches. If we dined at Martin's, it was I who addressed the waitress, asked for drinks *sin hielo*, and ordered for myself, for him. If anyone drove, it was I.

All around us, rocks of mountains soared to sky, and the city stretched into the vast Chihuahuan Desert. Spanish words flapped and rose and flew.

At the end of Matthew's visit, we stood in my *tíos'* garden, in between white walls and black fence, in between tenderness and uncertainty. In this part of the yard, no one could see us. I don't remember how we arrived there—if he asked me outside, if he pulled me gently from the house onto the bricked veranda and then onto the patch of grass. But alone, we faced each other. I imagine now the fig tree shifted slightly as Matthew—without ever posing any question, as if making a declaration—took my hand, limp at my side, lifted it, and tried to slide the ring he had brought onto my finger.

My heart thumped furiously.

The ring stuck halfway, and he pushed the solitaire harder against my knuckle. I shook my head and touched his arm—an arm I still loved with its muscles and freckles, a blend of man and boy—and told him, "I really meant it when I said I'm not ready."

Matthew looked at me, and his arms dropped to his sides. The corners of his mouth turned down, and his gaze fell to a place where I could not find it. I handed him the ring, and he shoved it back into his pocket. We stood frozen in that moment, in a place we'd been avoiding but now could not escape.

It was evening and raining, and my *tíos* were driving again, and all the cars in all the lanes clipped forward at a mighty speed. I sat alone in the back seat, only then beginning to sense the borders and ruptures of loss, even if loss is necessary to make the way forward clear. Outside, water slushed everywhere.

Then a dog—short-haired and lanky—darted out.

We could see it just ahead, motionless in front of us, but with lanes crowded on both sides and cars barreling behind us, there was nothing to do but keep rushing forward, our tires slicing the sloppy, soaking street.

The dog looked right at us, through the windshield and frantic wipers, just before we hit it with a thud.

For a horrifying five seconds—count them, they are long—the dog yelped, caught beneath our racing car. Trapped by wheels and chrome, its body knocked, smacked, battered right below where I sat in the back seat, stunned. Canine cries echoed against metal, and fur and bones clanked against the undercarriage. The dog rolled on and on and on.

When it was over, without a comment or acknowledgment, my uncle and aunt resumed their conversation—one I no longer wished to capture and hold, their Spanish language suddenly like a frail netting falling apart in my reaching hands.

I saw nothing but the road ahead, and the darkness of the car hovered, the city lights burned, and the traffic streamed onward down streets I could not name.

CHAPTER FOUR

The Compromise

It's entirely possible for your spirit to linger in a place even though you no longer live there. That's how I imagine it is in Yellow Springs, the Ohio village of four thousand where I grew up, where I think of myself as beginning, and in part, remaining. The green of Glen Helen shifts with the breeze near the heart of town, and swaths of farmland surround the village, as does a state park cut by a limestone gorge and waterfalls.

Yellow Springs is the place I returned to after graduate school, and again the year that followed my teaching stint in Torreón, and once more the seventeen months after I left my admissions job in Oxford, Ohio. It all went too fast. That was the last time I really lived in Yellow Springs, but it's a place I go back to as much as I can. It remembers me. It remembers who I was. But when you are young, you don't realize the price of decisions. There is a cost to everything because in choosing one thing, you un-choose another. It's why I like beginnings—that window of time when you can still go either way, when you have not yet faced giving up something you might love, something you might later regret having lost.

Luck finds you and it leaves you, though it's hard to say whether it is coming or going until later. Rob and I could have easily never met: we lived in the same place for so little time. He had just started graduate school, studying geography in Oxford at Miami University, where I was working but about to leave. I recruited students for admissions, going and returning in that red sedan, traveling to high schools and standing behind tables draped in red tablecloths at college fairs, trying to help seventeen-year-olds figure out what might make them happy when I, at twenty-seven, was not so sure myself.

Just before I met Rob, I had broken up with a man my family wanted me to marry. He had a beard and slender nose, and he was kind and good, the kind of good Catholic who did not believe in divorce, not just because of the church but because his heart comprised only entrances.

The day I was to break up, my sister called to try and stop me. Part of me knew my sister was right: that the man with the beard and the faith was the right choice at an awful time. I told him I shouldn't be dating anyone, and I was just as right as my sister. Not long before, he had taken me to see *The English Patient*, and I had wept afterward in the crowded restaurant, wept about Almásy having to leave Katharine in the dark and cold Cave of Swimmers, and wept about the line, "New lovers are nervous and tender, but smash everything. For the heart is an organ of fire." How could a line be so beautiful and true? I wept over that, too, and my good, Catholic man kept trying to comfort me, touched my arm, rubbed my back, but it was useless, for I had been weeping for months about everything and nothing. The day my sister called, I broke up with him in the cold of a car halfway between our houses.

I wanted out of Oxford, a tiny town with too little left for me, but just before I quit my job to move back to the hometown where I knew I belonged, my world collided with Rob's and then collapsed into it—though I did not know that at the time, could only see it looking back. This is what I saw:

One night, a February night, we drove with some friends into the heart of Cincinnati to the Corinthian—a Greek restaurant that stripped down to a salsa dance spot late at night. This was back when Rob and I had only just met and hardly knew each other. Everyone paid admission, showed IDs, and emerged into a dark dining room laced with cigarette smoke. A glow of soft white light ladled over the dancers swishing and wriggling on the dance floor. We shook off our coats and watched for a few minutes. I could tell Rob was eager to start dancing because he didn't sit still for long. "Come on," he said, motioning toward the dance floor.

Dancing can create a connection out of nothing, but I didn't know that then: I was a beginner. I didn't know how heady eye contact can be, how it can deceive, conjuring attraction and passion from air. If I had been an experienced dancer, I would have used more caution. I would have known how gaze-to-gaze creates a spider's strand that ensnares, and how a guiding touch—his hand pressed in the small of my back, a snap of his arm to spin me—casts a lulling spell, one that might not linger as long as its promise. There we were, swaying our hips, his palm against mine, his other hand pressed on my waist, my blouse thinning with sweat and seduction as he led me through the salsa's repeating rhythm. Physical touch, the feel of another's skin, tethers two people. On the dance floor, we were bound.

After a while we took a break, sitting side by side, and the silence—which I had noticed he could so easily fall into, which sometimes felt like emotional distance—seemed different then, as if wrapped around us, warming us from a cold world. The moment a slow song drifted from the speakers, Rob stood, turned to me, and reached out. We moved onto the dance floor, and he cloaked his arms around me. He smelled like soap and pine forests when he pulled me close—not so close we plastered against each other but enough so I could see the smooth basin of his neck and how easy it would be to rest there.

By the time we drove back to Oxford, I wanted to see him again. I forgot everything I had meant about not dating, or I remembered and pushed it aside—the faith, the cold car, my sister on the phone, telling me not to let go.

I forgot the heart was an organ of fire.

My old middle school is dark brick and windowless, and when I look at it all I see is my first kiss. Outside the school's front door, a boy named David kissed me when I was twelve. His lips grazed mine hurriedly as the final class bell rang—or was it I who hurried? The kiss terrified me, despite my huge crush on him. It seems now I always lagged behind other girls in being ready—for kissing, for sex, and later, for marriage.

Next to my old middle school is my high school, where in my senior year I came in second for everything: salutatorian, homecoming "senior attendant" (runner-up to Queen), honorable mention in the creative writing contest. Now, second feels fine, even good; it means you're nearly there, and it offers something that first does not: a second chance. Long ago, I stopped thinking first is best, that first has any bearing on worth.

Dayton Street—to the stoplight at the end of town and back to the barn where I grew up—is the one-mile strip I walked on with my parents and sister thousands of times, in shorts and t-shirts, in heavy coats and snow boots. We were always a family that walked together, abandoning our individual paces, my parents sometimes holding hands and pulling up the rear as my sister and I led. When we get the chance, we still do. On Dayton Street, people honk and wave at us, people we have known for decades.

Trees line the left side of South College Street, and on summer mornings, the sun lingers in the leaves. The light wells up in Gaunt Park, in its baseball fields and on the lush hill where the public swimming pool perches, the same pool where my friend Camilla and I spent the entire summer after sixth grade, our silver

season-pass pins worn faithfully as our skin darkened and we
tromped down the hill to the snack stand, oblivious of our changing bodies, before boys became big deals. *Easier, simpler*, I think
now. But perhaps what is simple is that I lump that time into such
a category, forgetting how I hated getting my first period, my first
bra, everything new hurtling at me.

Five months after our first dance at the Corinthian, Rob and I
stood side by side and leaned against a white sink in a hotel bathroom. With a brown paper bag between us filled with mangoes,
we dug a thumb into the red peel and pulled it back. We took
turns stripping peel and eating, scraping the flesh with our teeth.
The juice ran down our arms, sticky and sweet. The mango's
orange color was that of a late-day sun.

This was Acapulco, that first summer we were in love, on a
trip through the southernmost states of Mexico. Before arriving
in Acapulco, we had already lugged backpacks onto clean, cool
buses as well as overheated, congested buses, and one that
swerved unsteadily on a road carved out of a cliff. We had salsa
danced on a stone *zocalo* and sweated our way through beach
towns. We had climbed the ruins of Monte Albán.

I relied on Rob to haggle with hotel staff; he counted on
me to read maps. In Oaxaca, in a neighborhood of clapboard
houses that bent over with the weight of their roofs, a stray
dog had lunged at me, all wet teeth and snarl. Without hesitation, Rob planted himself between me and the growls and
shouted off the mutt.

After Acapulco, a fever drenched me in Taxco, and Rob ran out onto the dark, cobblestone streets at midnight for a thermometer and medicine from a twenty-four-hour pharmacy. By that time, I could not imagine a future without him.

In one of my journal entries during that trip, I wrote, "Rob said to write that he loves me." But he must have grabbed my pen because beneath it is scrawled—in his handwriting—"I love you," and then his signature.

In smaller letters below that, in parentheses, I wrote, "There, it's official."

For a long time, the mangoes, the mutt, the fever, and the journal entry were the stories I told myself. They were simple and true and lovely. I had a habit of saving what some people labeled sentimental and nostalgic. I kept the first gift I had ever gotten from a boyfriend years ago, a white Bundeswehr tank top that had begun to tear at the seams. In a shoebox, I stashed poems I had written and poems I had been given, even though the affection in the flowery words had long ago limped away. I was prone to remember the best and forget the breakups, the unanswered calls, the notes that said it's over, notes that could be folded up so tightly they might be mistaken for moths.

For a long time, I did not want to think about the other stories on our trip to Mexico: how Rob and I had not agreed on where to stay. Rob wanted hostels; I wanted AC and a bathroom without roaches scurrying every time I flipped on the light. We checked into cheap motels until Acapulco, when Rob gave in to a modest hotel with a small balcony. And later, we agreed on a former-monastery-now-inn, but by then I was sick—too ill to care.

And in Taxco, famous for its silver mines, I came up with the idea of our splitting up for an hour to buy each other silver gifts. I perused shop after shop of trinkets: jewelry, key chains, utensils. I finally settled on a man's ring, heavy but not ornate and with a jagged line zig-zagging around the band. I knew Rob would like it, and I could picture it on his finger, like a promise. I wondered what awaited me, but when we met up again on the stone central square as the sun brushed the horizon, the first thing he said was, "I didn't find anything for you, but I found something for me."

We had planned a four-week trip, but about halfway through I started to miss my hometown and my family. Back then I was not sure why. Not only had I traveled before, but I had lived abroad and never once wanted to up and leave and return to Ohio early. Now I understand that I felt a kind of unexpected loneliness, and it tinged the look of everything, making Huatulco not secluded but empty, tourists gone, a ghost town with a deserted beach. Later, I would remember Puerto Escondido as the place where waves slammed into sand so that all Rob and I could do was sit in rented plastic chairs, far from the water's fringes. A bloated fish blew onto shore, its jellied eye washed open.

Rob didn't argue when I said I wanted to go home after three weeks; he acquiesced but was annoyed, something he admitted much later. I might have known had I watched for signs: a quick inhalation of breath and a long exhalation, his eyes avoiding mine when I asked him, "Are you sure it's okay?"

I had not been searching back then for clues, for the things that might one day tear at the seams of our love. The only thing I knew was I wanted to go home. And now I can see clearly: he would never be that for me.

"Yellow Springs is too small," Rob said. This was after I had left Oxford and moved back to my hometown. This was after we were engaged, trying to figure out where to live after Rob graduated and we got married. The thought of bumping into people he knew while wheeling around a grocery cart made Rob cringe.

I had landed my dream job of recruiting students and writing publications for my alma mater near my beloved hometown, but I was not the type to insist or give ultimatums. I was more likely to believe in ever after. "I don't want to live in Seattle," I said of his hometown. "It's too far." I meant from my family, my town, the bones of my youth.

My parents still live in Yellow Springs in our converted barn. In 1973 my father walked into it for the first time and—before he and my mother saw the rest of it—turned to the realtor and said, "We'll take it." Just like that. He must have instantly fallen in love with the exposed wood beams and the light shafting down the stairwell from living room to yellow kitchen.

It was in that house that my sister and I built homes for our dolls in bookshelves, that we constructed make-shift tents by draping sheets over clusters of dining room chairs, and that we played hide-and-seek under beds and tables with our dog, Sable. In that kitchen, at the bottom of the steps, my mother sat beside me to teach me how to read, pointing to words and sounding them out for me. Within those walls, my father taught me how to defend myself, how to make a fist and hit the boy who bullied me at school. It was in the house's laundry room, when I was sixteen, that Sable's hips gave out one last time, and it was in our den, under the orange glow of stain-glassed windows, that I kissed Ben, my four-year-long crush, for the first time.

The house didn't just hold my family's history: it changed with us. It shed its shag carpet for Italian tile; it lengthened by two bedrooms and a screened-in porch; it widened its windows and grew a golden transom above the back door. Somehow, that house and I grew up together.

What about San Francisco, Rob said.

What about somewhere else in Ohio, I said.

A few months before we were to marry, I made Rob sit next to me on the edge of my bed. "I understand if you need to live on the West Coast," I told him, "but if you do, then we really shouldn't get married." I made myself look him in the eye when I said it.

"No, no," Rob said. He took my hand. "I can be happy anywhere."

But anywhere never included Ohio. Rob had only gone there to get his master's degree, not to remain. He would not consider Columbus or Cincinnati—he wanted to work with Latino migrant workers, and back then Ohio did not draw Central Americans looking for jobs. Later I would wonder if that was the entire truth. Maybe staying in Ohio felt like competition with my family, and he wanted us to have a fresh start, just the two of us. Maybe he hated

Ohio with its flat acres of corn and soybeans, those green, unfurling, summer fields I dreamed of every time I left.

Eventually, we settled on Chapel Hill, North Carolina. The town had a growing Latino population, universities where I might work, and it was within driving distance of Yellow Springs.

But while Rob looked forward to leaving Ohio—a state he could not live within—I looked back at everything I did not know if I could live without.

As I grew up, my mother was the sound of applause: at my screeching viola concerts, at my choir recitals when I belted out ballads, at my poetry readings even after I rushed through words as if they were tornadoes drilling across the page. I orbited around my mother's clapping hands.

Two years before I met Rob, when I first started recruiting students for Miami University, I had to travel ten weeks in a row in the fall. I returned on Friday nights to my apartment in Oxford, only to leave again early on Sunday mornings. The Ohio highways unraveled into horizon. By week eight, the last of autumn left the trees naked and thin. The fields, shorn of crops, stretched brown and endless from the two-lanes and four-lanes and from all those country roads. The hotel rooms began to feel like caves. That's when I confessed to my mother that the loneliness was taking its toll, and I did not want to go. We both knew I would: commitments kept me cemented in my decisions.

"I'll go with you," my mother said without hesitating. I imagined my mother packing a small bag: a blue comb, a cloth sack of colored curlers, stockings, a silky blouse, one pair of shoes, lotion for her hands.

On the way to Toledo and Detroit, I drove to pick her up, and together we took the sedan north, my mother's chatter enveloping and warming the car, making it shelter. Each night, my mother slept in the hotel bed beside me, her small figure huddled under the covers, her rise and fall the only way I breathed.

With a string of high schools to visit each day, I had to leave early in the morning, sometimes at 6:30 a.m. to make it to the first stop. My mother, in pressed slacks and a boiled wool sweater with brass buttons, stalked out of the room right behind me, clutching a stack of crossword puzzles, a book, a black ink pen. I parked on the edges of school lots and then made my way to glass entrances and through hollow hallways that would crash with students in between classes. When I emerged an hour later from fluorescent light to sun, I saw my mother even from a distance, even when rows of white lines and wide asphalt spanned the space between us in the lot. I saw my mother's black hair and olive skin past the shiver of glass, her face bent over as if praying, intent on sorting out words or scanning magazines.

My mother looked up when I got close. She always looked up.

She smiled and waved as I approached, as if we had not seen each other an hour ago. As if I were brand new.

At the corner of downtown Yellow Springs, where Limestone Street crosses Xenia Avenue, one of five village stoplights winks yellow late at night. Right at that corner is the one-room public library, every brick of it unchanged since I shelved books as a library page throughout high school and until I left for college. I still wear the scarlet and black scarf the librarians gave me for graduation. It reminds me of work I loved—the alphabetizing, the order of it all, the way I could empty a cart quickly, sliding hardbacks and paperbacks into their slots, back where they were meant to be. I liked the librarians, and they liked me. It was the first place that, outside of my family, I was trusted, counted on, given tasks but not overly managed, and at some points not managed at all. I liked this sense—however small being charged with books is—of responsibility, of not slacking, of being useful.

Of being depended on to do the right thing.

I remember the first time Rob and I fought, when we were still dating, still living an hour apart. He went out with friends one night until late without telling me, even though I'd told him I would call at eleven. It was our nightly ritual to talk, especially because of the distance and seeing each other only on weekends, but he hadn't tried to get back in time for the call, and though he phoned the next morning and said he was sorry, I held onto the hurt—I was prone to such holdings—and said the phone call didn't mean enough to him. I wouldn't have cared had he said, "Don't call, I have plans," but he had said nothing, and nothing seemed to me like an endless grey sky, portending rain or drizzle, clouds that closed off blue and stars and dazzle. Already the balance was tipping, but the next day we met halfway between his place and mine and said *I'm sorrys*, *I love yous*, frightened at the idea that something so small could knock us from the middle place we thought could last a lifetime.

The second time we fought was two months before we married, except this time we did not meet halfway. My former boyfriend Matthew had asked me to try again, and though I said no, there were a few days and weeks that followed when a different light fell on Rob's face, on mine. I saw shadows I had not seen before. It was a time I began to ask him how much he loved me, but I asked him obliquely: if he lived far away from me, would he travel from several states away just to see me, even if only for a day? He bristled at my questions: "Why are you asking me this?" And I had closed my eyes and told myself to stop, that his love was plain—no frills, no fuss—but solid: I was getting married after all. I did not blurt out anything; I held the panic in like breath. Even then I knew I was asking whether his love was enough—for marriage? For moving? For all of it.

But I realize now I was also asking if mine was.

For a long time, I didn't tell anyone what happened on our honeymoon. It seemed like a thin sort of secret, so meaningless and small it could slip from the world without notice.

One morning in Montreal, as we walked down a street and then crossed another, I must have said something to annoy Rob —maybe asked him to tell me he loved me?—because he said in response he felt smothered.

My eyes shot to him. My feet froze in place. My heart thrashed in its cage.

"I didn't mean it how it sounded," he said.

"What *did* you mean?" I asked.

"I just meant…" He hesitated. He blinked a few times, shook his head. "I don't know. I'm sorry."

"You should have married someone else," I said to him, but now I think I meant I should have. Rob apologized more, and when I wouldn't look him in the eye, he fell into the kind of silence that if it were a color would be purple, like a bruise.

We both kept on. Our feet thudded against the sidewalk. Our arms didn't touch though we trudged side by side. I'm sure I was the one who did not let them. It took hours of walled silence—during which I didn't give him long answers, didn't ask him questions, didn't reach out to hold his hand—before I let it drop.

That afternoon, in the dwindling light, when the sun fell on the sides of buildings as if it were running down the walls instead of shining on them, Rob said he wanted to rest a bit at the B&B. We returned to our room that by then seemed smaller than when we had left it. I said I'd be back and left him motionless, alone on the bed. Maybe that's what he wanted. He must have felt drained from trying to smooth things over. Maybe he didn't really know how to not hurt me. It feels that way now, that we knew so little about each other.

He wanted to sleep. I wanted to walk. I wanted to run, really, but I ambled from our B&B to a public garden some blocks away. The waning light looked like fading gold. I thought about my family, how far away they seemed, and how equally far away they would be when we moved to North Carolina. What had I done?

A feeling of dread—that months earlier had crawled and coiled into my stomach—now rattled, now hissed.

At that moment, I realized it was Matthew I wanted to call, Matthew whose voice I wanted to hear. When we had been in love, his commanding presence, his assuredness—things that sometimes made me feel overpowered—had so often calmed me and made me feel that I could rest when beside him. I know now that what I really wanted was something I glimpsed setting over the horizon, dying in the amber sky: a sense of security. But in my panic, I only knew I wanted to hold onto something that felt more sturdy than what I saw before me.

I sought a pay phone on the street and found one under the shelter of an overhang. I punched in my calling card code to make the call and then dialed the numbers I knew by heart. When my mother picked up, I pretended everything was okay. I was good at pretending, moving on. I tried to forget it was Matthew I wanted to call. It was one of the first brave things I did in my young marriage—not lean on the idea of someone else when I wanted to, or at least, not for long. I was only beginning to understand that strong marriages are not simply handed out to those who think they deserve them: they are earned. I knew I had a choice, and I wanted to make it well.

Rob and I left the incident behind us as if promises could be bent and still not break. We showered together, letting the days rinse off us. We held hands before we fell asleep, letting go only as we drifted away. New marriages can have such fragile fences. We took a train elsewhere, to different streets, ones on which we had not argued: we traveled to Quebec City, paved with brick, shouldered by stone homes, a city filled with things hard enough to contain us and our new marriage, soft and formless. On cobblestone streets, we looked for a bar where we might go dancing, and we let the beat move our weary arms and legs, let music fill the space around us so we did not need any words. Back then I thought that was bravery, but I think now it was denial. I thought being brave meant not looking too far into the future, not imagining the worst, or at least pretending I did not. But if I had been brave, I would have run.

In the years that followed, I didn't tell anyone what Rob had said about my love smothering him, the panic I felt after, that perhaps Rob felt, too, and I certainly never told anyone I wanted to call a former love first, not my mother. I excused it as a momentary unguarded thought, yet hadn't Rob's comment been that, too? The only difference is I had not said mine out loud.

But here I am saying it: I wanted to call Matthew. I wanted everything back I had given up. I wanted to go home.

Now, blinking back at me in memory, Rob looks the way he did when we first met, hair a rich and dark black, and that face, smooth and round. When he did not know what to say, or was mulling something over, he blinked instead of spoke.

For some years, I could not recall his face, but now I remember him: he stands in his galley kitchen, making me tea for the first time, stirring a tea bag in hot water in a mug that matches no others in his tiny kitchen, in his damp basement apartment.

This is before we have started dating, when we barely know each other.

This is before Mexico, and before our summer trip to Seattle when we will stay in his old room with twin beds at his parents' place in Bellevue and sleep with the windows open and without screens, and we will squeeze into one bed for the first hours of every night and hold each other as if we'll never part.

We have not yet fast-danced to George Michael in Rob's living room or slow-danced to Luis Miguel in mine. It's before we've salsa-danced in clubs and anywhere we can push a couch and coffee table aside to make room to synchronize our steps, to learn each other's signals and strengths, to know each other's moves so well it will become hard to dance with anyone else.

This is when I only know that we both have Latina mothers (his, from Ecuador; mine, from Mexico) but not that we share other things: a love of forests, lakes, and an earnest sun; a belief in liberal politics, religious freedom, and living within our means.

This is before he's told me that he was the first in his nuclear family to earn a bachelor's degree and thus the first to go to graduate school, before I know he had never set foot on the campus in Oxford before arriving to start his first fall semester. Leaving his parents and sister in Seattle, he flew solo to Oxford and slept in a van for two nights while apartment-hunting. When he found a place, though it was damp and cold, he moved in, accepting it without complaint. He will not tell me this so I will think of him as brave, though I will. He will state it as fact, as if to say: *This is who I am. I'm not afraid to be alone. I'm not afraid of change.*

This is before I know he pickets causes and refuses to buy from companies he deems irresponsible, before he has boycotted a large pickle company until it gives its undocumented workers safe and clean housing. This is before I know he fights for the rights of people he sees as "have-nots," especially poor Latino immigrants, and before I know he abhors anything that smacks of upper-crust or upper-class. This is before he knows my family is upper middle-class. This is before he knows I might have innocently and ignorantly bought the pickles from the bad company.

This is before love.

As he stirs my tea, the spoon clatters against the mug's side. Then he stops, and the room is quiet, not yet filled with shared joys or sorrows or too much hope. We can still say goodbye without hurting.

Rob's apartment is barely furnished—all I see are two director chairs in his living room. The chairs have red canvas backs, but their main structures are a soft and light wood, likely pine, that cannot mask nicks and dents and scratches. These are the chairs that weeks later we will push aside to make room for falling in love. Just two chairs. I do not care that he does not own things, that he has a bike but no car, a mattress but no bed frame, chairs but no table. He is a man of possibility, a blank page where I might fill in the rest. It will not occur to me until years later that he might not want to be filled in at all, that he might like for half of his heart to be empty, for the other half to be free. That for me his heart might be a heart of exits.

Maybe I can see Rob's face so clearly now because it has been more than a decade since I loved him. Maybe that's why I can conjure up this moment—the first time he made me tea, when I was upset about something that had happened at work and went to his basement apartment because it was the one thing I thought would comfort me, though he was nearly a stranger. We sat with our unmatching mugs, and he did not ask me to talk about whatever had upset me. He let me be, and I thought of this as kind. He let me be, as he would years later when he told me our marriage was over: I was sitting on the green futon I had lugged around for longer than our marriage, and he was sitting in one of two chairs my parents had given us, chairs I would later give back. I wept into my hands as if they were pages of a book I would never get to read. Rob did not get up to comfort me. He watched, as he had that day in his basement apartment. He let me be. It did not feel kind then, in our Chapel Hill living room, with the vertical blinds of the patio door shaking when the heat rose from the vent below. The metal slats slapped against each other as the furnace tried to warm this coldest of rooms.

But now I do not think Rob was being unkind. He was as he had always been, only by that time, after those years, I had filled in the things he did not want to have filled. I had placed a mortgage document where he wanted only a passport—a thing that would never tether him to a place. I had bugged him for closeness and physical affection where he wanted alone time and personal space. I had too often finished his sentences. I had too often said I love you. I had too often believed that if I could just make him love me more, he might want other things less: as soon as we moved to Chapel Hill, he wanted to move again—to Boston, Seattle, San

Francisco—and it only occurred to me later that it might not have been about the place he was running to, but about the person he was running from.

I close my eyes and watch as Rob stirs sugar into my tea, back in his Oxford apartment, and puts the mug again into my cupped hands as if we are starting over. I remember this, our beginning, but I no longer know if it was also our end.

On a hot August day, one month after we married, we hauled the last of my things out to the moving truck in Yellow Springs, and I began the leaving.

My parents and sister raised their hands as they stood by the door, all of them waving vigorously, as if wiping the air clean. I held onto their three figures in the rearview mirror until I pulled away from the gravel alley next to the house to follow the beastly moving truck, driven by Rob, as it lurched and rumbled down Winter and then Dayton Street, jerked through the stoplight at the Tastee Freeze, dug into the road, and hunched toward Route 68, away from Yellow Springs, and, eventually, toward North Carolina.

I gripped the steering wheel hard, as if holding on meant never letting go.

Rob and I had walkie-talkies, and we clicked out messages to each other, indicating bathroom breaks, right exits, thirst. At one point, a downpour hissed onto us, forcing us to pull over. I saw Rob through the steamed windows—I in the car, he in the truck—and he looked so far away. I tried to glimpse home in his pale, round face, to see it through two windows and the jagged slant of rain.

The world blurred between us, and Rob held the chunky walkie-talkie to his ear, even when we had nothing to say.

CHAPTER FIVE

The Last Kiss

Rob and I conceived the idea: meet on January 1 at the Charlotte airport from our separate starting points; together, fly the last leg home to Chapel Hill. When we thought it up—months before it was to happen—the idea had swelled with joy. But that first day of the new year, when we actually had to execute the plan, it sagged under the weight of everything we had decided since booking our tickets: namely, that we were divorcing.

By virtue of the fact that he wanted out and I wanted in, I admit I am unlikely to tell this story fairly. It won't be generous enough toward him, but it will be the truth of how I saw it then.

Before the decision to end our marriage, Rob had wavered for weeks about what he wanted. I realize now that he must have been struggling with his opposing wishes, but I resented him for the juggle and resented myself, too, for I was still grappling with my own mythology: that my actions had the power to make him choose to stay and that my worth was tied up in his choices. "Let's pretend we've decided to get divorced," he proposed one night, "just not tell anyone and see how it feels," as if the demise of our marriage were something he could return if it did not suit him. He said this just after Thanksgiving, which we had spent with my family without mentioning how our love teetered on the edge of the abyss.

"I'm not pretending anything," I said. "Just tell me when you know."

But twenty-four hours later, when Rob said he knew, I did pretend, or at least I said nothing to my two closest friends at work the next morning. I gripped the white wooden banister as I climbed the stairs to my office, and I kept my door half-shut. The light bled through my windows, and I made small talk only when someone pushed the door wider and leaned in to find me. My two friends might have known because my face was pulled into a knot, but I kept my wedding band on until the afternoon sky darkened. Then I called my two friends in, shut the door, and told them my marriage was over. In the days that followed, every time I told someone, I was letting the words—*you have failed, you chose wrong, you were never enough*—fall into step beside me. I was too tired to outrun them anymore.

Rob and I had planned to celebrate our "Christmas" together in early December and then each travel to see our parents for the twenty-fifth—he in Seattle, I in Yellow Springs—and return at the start of the new year to the home we had made for ourselves three and half years earlier in North Carolina.

The plan had seemed sweeter, nothing like a burden, before the divorce decision.

On January 1, I exited my plane and ambled toward the Charlotte airport's food court where I had agreed to wait for Rob. My stomach tumbled round and round. I knew I would not be hungry: I had already started shedding weight, every food looking as though it should be pushed away. Eventually, in the weeks that followed, I would lose fourteen pounds.

At the airport food court, in the atrium, travelers rested their heads against the backs of rocking chairs. These chairs, with their thick wood painted white, were meant to make the airport feel warm, like home, but instead it felt like someone was trying to trick me out of noticing the shine on the floors or the gleam of steel beams criss-crossing the night sky.

My husband, who was also supposed to feel like home, would be moving out of our condo the following day. I had reasoned it would be easier for Rob rather than for me to leave, as he valued change and adventure over the kind of predictability and sameness I sought and grasped. Rob had already started the legal proceedings for the dissolution of our marriage. He sent me the papers while I was in Ohio, and I clutched the pen and pressed my name into them, into the small underlined spaces where I did not belong.

This had prompted me to run in the winter ache of my hometown, farther than I thought possible, past Duncan Park with

its naked crabapple trees and vacant picnic table, by Gaunt Park
pool emptied of hot and sweet summer, and below a sky so thick
and grey I could not see the sun. I ran in downpours that pelted
my skin with a cold that stung and, in its stinging, soothed.

These were the kinds of opposites I was learning to live with.

The last time Rob and I had spoken was December 25, when he
called my parents' house to wish me and my family a merry Christmas—and to talk to me about the King County documents that
would be filed and stamped by clerks who would never know me.

"I think you're making the biggest mistake of your life," I
blurted out.

Lord knows that was not a way to win back a man's heart, but I
had not been attempting that. Grief had become a liquor that sup-
pressed my inhibitions and left me stumbling, acting from nonsensical conclusions: that if he hurt more, I might hurt less; that even
though I was sure there was nothing he could say to win me back, I
wanted him to try. Maybe, more than anything, I wanted to see him
fail the way I thought I had failed at saving our marriage.

"I've wanted to talk to you every day," Rob said. They were
holding-on kinds of words. Then he added, "But I didn't want to
upset you by calling."

"It's hard to hear from you," I said. "I'm dreading going back
and having you move out." The grief burned down my throat,
and I winced at this admission.

"Will it be easier after I've left?" he asked.

And there it was, a circle back to where we had started: the

King County documents, the clenching in my chest, running in the winter rain.

"Yes," I said, "it will."

I was not leaning forward as we sat across from each other at a table too small for us and all our baggage. The smell of food—grilled, baked, sautéed—wafted the air.

The marriage was over for me, just not in feeling, and I was tangled in a world of wanting impossibilities: to go back in time and change everything; to go forward in time and never look back.

I shifted the conversation to a place where I did not have to really pay attention. My mind wandered as we talked about the small things in our lives that used to matter but by then felt like clutter. I tried to conjure up the place I had been the week before, sitting in a cold car outside my parents' house in the middle of the block where I grew up, with an old friend who had come to visit.

This friend and I had spent the evening catching up, lying next to the Christmas tree as if we were looking up at the stars, the white lights blinking down onto his blue eyes, dark sweater, and his long legs, in jeans, stretched out before him. The strands of silver tinsel dangled near our faces. He had arrived in the afternoon and stayed for dinner with my family—he was someone I had known for over a decade, that my family knew, too, and we had kept in touch and were close, though thousands of miles stretched like cords over the mountains and plains between our cities. We tried to see each other most Christmases when we both returned to our home state of Ohio. It never felt like reconnecting. It felt more like tugging taut what hung loose between us the rest of the year.

We had already talked about the breakdown of my marriage by phone (he had coaxed me out of the shadow of sadness more than once), and that night he made me laugh, as he always could, especially when he put on an accent—of an Englishman or what I thought of as a thug from Little Italy. But it was even better when he made himself laugh, when he threw his head back a little, reminding me of a kind of freedom I had lost in the previous months, a freedom that might be possible again.

After dinner, and after talking more alone, he said he had to go. We stood up together, and then he declared, matter-of-factly, that before he left he was going to kiss me, but I was not sure what he meant—on the cheek? Was it a joke? We had not kissed in years, having survived our college romance of several months by settling into an abiding friendship in the years that followed.

We walked out of my parents' house, unlatching the gate and taking the slim sidewalk to where he had parked, enveloped in darkness. I got into his car to escape the unrelenting cold while he flipped the key in the ignition to let the engine and the interior warm up for his drive home. It was late, and I could feel the lateness in my body, as if I could go limp at any moment. Through the windshield my old neighborhood looked blank, not just because the street was void of cars and people but because the sweep of night can canvas the world into a kind of emptiness.

When the car was warm enough, I hugged him goodbye and turned away to find the door handle. That's when he reached over, tugged me to him, and kissed me. He was a smoker, but he had covered it up throughout the day with gum or a mint (not to hide the truth but out of courtesy to me, a non-smoker), and his lips felt warm and tasted sweet, the way I remembered young love could be. I did not protest the kiss—well, I thought of protesting it, realizing I was still married and there was probably some rule or line I should not be crossing, but I could not remember the last time I'd been kissed with such tenderness.

Finally I pulled back and said, "I shouldn't be doing this."

"Why?"

"Because I'm not in a place to be doing this." I was trying to remind him I was emotionally unfit. My face looked longer from so little food, my hair tangling and thin, my complexion blotchy, but earlier he had said—he always said—I was beautiful, and that evening, in that car, I wanted to believe it.

"I don't want to hurt you," I said.

For a moment he said nothing. Then he smiled. We had lived so far from each other for so long that we were an impossibility—we had both known that for over a decade. Which is why that kiss was possible: that we could both lean in, and, for a moment, both let go.

Rob doesn't love you anymore. It was this thought I inhaled deeply in the food court, a smell that permeated the walls and made me nauseous and unsteady.

"So when are you moving back to Seattle?" I blurted out.

Rob looked up from his plate of food, fork poised in his hand. His green eyes blinked. "I don't know," he said. "That all depends."

"On what? Your job?" I was talking in clipped sentences. I had become less polite in the leaving.

"Yes," he said. "And also on what happens with us."

A shouting struck up in my head: *Ask him what he means. Does he think you're getting back together? Ask him, ask him.* But my pride shushed the shouting, and the only words that fumbled out were, "You did file the papers, didn't you?"

"Yes," he said, "but it's only $120."

Here was yet another thing to want but to know was impossible. The wrenching in my stomach told me not to press him.

Rob and I walked together to our gate. People hurried past us and around us, our two bodies a slow boat in a sea of travelers rushing back to their lives. Usually I rushed too, but this was the last leg on our journey together, and I hated myself for wanting to slow it down.

When we arrived at the gate, an airline attendant announced our flight was oversold. Anyone who volunteered to give up a seat would get a free ticket and be bused to Chapel Hill that night.

Rob's face brightened, and I knew before he told me that he was volunteering to give up his seat.

"It's a free ticket," he said. "Aren't you?"

I looked into the green eyes of the man I still loved but did not want to. He was looking me straight in the eye in the exact way he could not just months earlier, long before the decision, when we had both sat on our bed, legs dangling over the edge, and he had said he loved me but then added, "But I'm not sure I'm *in* love with you anymore."

Those were leaving words, though I did not know it then. I feel foolish now for what I missed. I still believed in chances, in counseling, and the old American dream that if you work hard enough, you can succeed. Instead, in the weeks that followed, we had whittled away what we had, listing off each other's failures until our marriage became a flimsy thing.

And then there we were, standing at the airport at the end of all the choices we had made along the way, and this person—who was at that moment still my husband but very soon would not be—was asking me if I wanted to go with him, if I wanted a free ticket, too. And this, out of everything, seemed the most impossible.

When I think back to that moment and conjure up the green eyes and dark hair of the man I loved then, I see him—even understand him and his struggles—more clearly than I could that day in the airport. Now I understand Rob was a man who could never pass up a free ticket. That piece of paper represented new experience and possibility, two things he prized. As the years passed, when I thought of him, I pictured him dressed in one of his favorite t-shirts, the one with a black-bereted Che Guevara, the face of a revolution. Rob became so many things I remembered better, later: a man who longed to see Cuba; a man who once told me he wanted to move to South America, even when he knew I did not want to; a man who fought for the rights and freedoms of undocumented Latinos in the US; a man who, in the end, rebelled against our marriage, a thing that abolished his freedoms. It took me a long time to see that months before that moment in the airport, even before the divorce decision, before I ever knew, he was drunk in his own sort of grief, stumbling, acting from nonsensical conclusions: that he might somehow let go of all the things in our marriage that felt oppressive and at the same time still hold onto me.

Maybe in his grief that day at the airport, he was learning to live with his own set of opposites: that he might still love me yet still let me go.

The hours to our last day were dwindling. He was waiting for my answer.

It would have been so easy to turn in my airline reservation and agree to the promise of a free ticket, a new adventure, but my throat thickened, and I swallowed and shook my head. "No," I said. "I just want to get home."

"But it's a free ticket."

I nodded and said, "I know."

Later, when Rob got home—which was late, after midnight—I was not lying awake waiting for him as I had done before when he would go out with friends. On those nights, before crawling into bed with me, he had always showered, had let the cigarette smoke from the bars run from him because he knew I hated the smell and did not want it dirtying our sheets. But the last time he had come home from a night out with friends—had it been summer? early fall?—he had started to pull back the sheet even though he was wrapped in a cloud of smoke and stale beer. When I had protested, he said, "I'm too tired to shower," and fell into bed decidedly, the way he might have done had he been single, throwing the covers over his shoulders, settling in and saying nothing more.

He did not kiss me.

He did not smell like mint.

He drifted off to sleep, as if I were not there.

CHAPTER SIX

The Curious Thing about Doubt and Faith

In the early mornings of the spring I turned twenty-nine, the season before I married Rob, I drove on a stretch of Ohio's Route 68 to work I loved. I liked it best when the road showed up for me alone, when I could steer in a kind of solitary silence from village to rural county, from Epic Books and Ha Ha Pizza to the intersection with Cemetery Road, and then past pastures, swaths of farmland, and the occasional framed house onto which the sunlight warmed the lives of families rising into day. I had known the road for so long—not just the yawn of corn and soybean fields but also Young's Jersey Dairy with its red barn and white fence; Ebenezer Cemetery with its crumbling cement wall; the turnoffs for Sparrow, Collier, and Cottingham roads; even Walt's, the junkyard, where the highway doglegged. Yet that spring I studied each moment of the way as if remembering it well meant some-how I could keep it.

Back then, I wanted to believe in beginnings, but I can see now I held on to the ends.

Corazón: the Spanish word for heart. The admissions receptionist, Joann, had scrawled the international student's name—Mateo Corazón—next to mine on the interview sheet for later that morning.

"With me?" I asked Joann. Another Wittenberg University admissions officer typically handled foreign applicants.

"He said he was from Torreón, Mexico," she said. "He asked for you."

"Because I know Spanish?" I asked and then thought of my Tía Tela and Tío René. "Does he know my family?"

Joann shrugged.

"Well," I said, "I'd better get ready." I plucked brochures and an international application from the shelves and settled in at my desk.

I had worked in this very office from my freshman year until college graduation and then returned years later to my alma mater for full-time work. But in three months, I would be giving up the job, my hometown, my home state—places where I belonged—for that move to Chapel Hill. I cannot blame Rob for the fact that I had acquiesced to leaving, even though my chest tightened when I thought about it. When I was twenty-nine, I believed that surrendering what I wanted for the sake of someone else was the cost of love and that I should bear it.

Through my office wall, I could hear Joann's muffled voice mingled with a deeper one. Apparently, Mateo Corazón had shown up early. I was sitting at my desk, talking on the phone, my back to my door when I heard it open and Joann say, "You can sit down. She'll just be a minute." I always met prospective students out in the lobby, but I hurried off my call, and only after hanging up did I swing my chair around and rise—

I froze.

From his chair, Matthew rose, too, like an apparition ascending from memory.

For the appointment, as a ruse (and to back up his false claim of hailing from Mexico), Matthew had used the Spanish version of his first name, and Corazón in place of his last.

I had been twenty-four when I had fallen in love with Matthew. He was the only man I had been happy and eager to follow anywhere, even across or out of the country if he had so wished, just so we would never be apart. I spent much of the first six months of our relationship longing not just for a ring but to come before the stack of priorities standing between me and first place: his research, post-graduate school goals, his life plan that only vaguely—perhaps later—included me. After I moved back from Torreón, months after he attempted to give me a ring in my aunt's garden, I turned away from him entirely, no longer sure of who I was or what I wanted. It was easier for me, by then a mere twenty-five years old, to move on alone than to figure all that out with him.

But in the years that followed, when I was twenty-six and twenty-seven and living in Oxford, Ohio, Matthew had shown up. One time he drove eight hours from Washington, DC, through a snowstorm to see me; another time, when I was lonely and depressed, he drove two hours from his hometown in Indiana, where he was staying for the summer, to take me salsa dancing. He wrote me letters even when we had just talked or seen each other. Over the years he had given me a book of Neruda love poems, a picture frame with blue flowers pressed beneath glass, a bird feeder. His biggest gift, though, was a sacrifice: Matthew put off a semester of his PhD program in Nebraska to live closer to me. He had gone to great lengths to show me I came first, but I had told myself, repeatedly and with admonition, *only foolish girls believe a man will change.*

Until he showed up in my office on that warm and clear May day.

Matthew stood before me and grinned, clearly proud of having flown in from Nebraska to surprise me. We had been in contact, but eighteen months had passed from the time we had last seen each other to the moment Joann led him to me. My hands trembled because I was happy to see him—and aware I should not be. He knew about my engagement. This fact stood between us, arms folded across its chest, and shook its head.

The best I could blurt out was, "What are you doing here?"

He laughed. "I wanted to see you."

Later, when a cool-headedness prevailed, I said, "If you're here to change my mind, I won't."

He did not hesitate or blanch. His impeccable posture alerted the world that this man held few if any doubts about anything he set his mind to. "I only want to see what is possible," he said. Then he asked me to lunch.

In the brightness of the late morning light, we walked across campus to the student center café and found a table by a wall of windows. We laughed and lingered as if we were undergraduates and had all the time in the world for big choices and hard lines, as if none of those things mattered now. Later, we rambled around Wittenberg, eventually settling on a bench overlooking Myers Hollow, near the slope I had slipped down after an ice storm my freshman year before smacking into a tree.

For a minute we stared out onto the hollow.

Ever fearless, he broke the silence. "Marry me," he said. He reached into his pocket and pulled out the same ring he had, four years earlier, offered me. Except now, instead of a diamond in the setting, a green stone the size and color of a pea perched on top.

As he waited for my answer, I studied him: his blue eyes I remembered squinting at me in the dim morning light before he would reach for his glasses; his freckles that faded, forgotten in winter, but that would sprinkle across his nose and cheeks when flushed out by summer sun; his bushy brown hair, unruly after sleep, that could be tamed with water and a comb.

Finally, I said, "I can't."

"I don't believe you," he whispered, almost to himself.

"I won't," I said. The words tasted metallic.

We sat in silence and let the sun break against us on our

bench, let the gap—between now and his flight back to Nebraska, between now and my future husband and married life in North Carolina—become a little narrower.

Then we ambled, taking the long way back along the hollow's edge toward the place he had parked. We descended via a tree-lined path veiling us in shadow and emerged into the glare of sun and asphalt. When we embraced goodbye, I held onto him longer than he held onto me, and when I stepped away and toward Recitation Hall, toward my office and the life I knew, I had to force myself to do so, to train my eye on the glass door and push the metal bar that spanned it, to go through and not look back.

He left me the little gold ring with its pea stone, and it burrowed into my pocket, planting itself deep: a seed of doubt that would grow and grow.

It was three and half years later in late and cold November that my marriage disintegrated into the 50 percent statistic I had sworn I'd never belong to. It would be a lie to say I had been in love with my ex-boyfriend during my marriage to Rob because I had not, but Matthew's big love and big gestures had become the ruler against which I—however unfairly—had measured every disagreement with my husband, every incident in which I did not feel loved enough. I mourned not just my impending divorce but what might have been had I only chosen differently.

Matthew had moved from Nebraska to North Carolina, but I found this out only weeks before the divorce decision. I discovered through someone else, not from him, that he lived only twenty-five minutes away.

In late November, I wanted to go right to him, but the grief of my marriage ending clouded and rumbled in my chest. I knew, too, that grief passes, that it is only weather in the vast sky of the heart.

In January, I asked Matthew to come over. He showed up with a loaf of bread he had kneaded and baked for me, with all the ingredients he still remembered I loved: whole grains, seeds and nuts, and plump, black raisins. Just as he had years earlier, he took me to a salsa club, and I clung to his hand when he twirled me as if we could wind back to where we had stopped, and start again. Just as before, he gave me gifts: a white cotton top with three-quarter sleeves and a buttonhole neckline; a bouquet of gardenias whose fragrance wafted from my front stoop; a white colander to shake out unwanted water; a brown umbrella with faces of dachshunds and cocker spaniels splashed across the fabric. But unlike before, he had become born-again, and now he threaded Bible verses into emails and letters and tried to stitch me back together with Jesus's words.

Although my spirituality was private and quiet and rested in a God who favored heart over creed, I did not say no when he asked to pray out loud with me; I did not say stop when he offered biblical passages as balms. I wanted to believe in our beginning.

Without the physical intimacies and commitment of real couples —because of his religion, and because I was still emotionally reeling from the divorce—we became, still, devoted to each other. I drove him to Lasik surgery and nervously thumbed through magazines in the waiting room. I helped haul his truckload of furniture into his new house, and together we painted a clean coat on the walls. It was he who steered the car through hordes of I-95 traffic to whisk me to DC for a weekend and to point out landmarks and pick restaurants. It was he who rubbed my back the day I officially divorced, when I wept face down on the bed, boring into a pillow. And it was he who sat beside me as the mortgage broker shuffled refinance papers across the desk for me to sign, the pages stacked like a book I could not bear to read alone.

God, I loved him. He resurrected me.

But our differences sank into my belly. At night I felt them, cold and hard and unmoving. I thought the world was too big for only one religion, so we argued about how many paths led to God, and interpreting the Bible literally. I also conjured up hypothetical questions to test how he would prioritize his beliefs in relation to me. I know now I was really testing his love. I asked inane questions like, "If you and I were married, and you believed God wanted you to go live in Africa, even if it meant leaving me behind, would you go?"

In the end, he always said he would have no choice but to do whatever he thought God or Jesus wanted him to do but that God would not ask him to do something that would harm our relationship.

You're stirring up trouble, I chided myself, and for a while I stopped peppering him with questions to which I did not want to know his answers.

Then one night over the phone I prodded more about his beliefs, poking a fire I knew I could not contain if the flames leapt. I thought about all of my gay and lesbian friends, and I jabbed the topic open.

He told me that homosexuality was a sin, and I asked him how he could make such a judgment. He said he was not making that judgment: God was. Suddenly, I wanted to dampen all of it, and I flooded him with questions until I found a concocted safe and middle ground: yes, he loved all people, straight or gay, and though he did not think gay couples should be able to get married or adopt, yes, he thought all people were equals.

Though I cried when we hung up the phone and lost my appetite for a day and a half, I clung to the word "equals." I reminded myself he had always been nothing short of welcoming and warm to all of my friends, and I convinced myself the place where he stood and where I stood were not so far apart, that if we both leaned toward each other, we could still touch.

It was spring by then, the season of possibility.

This was not the first time our views had clashed, that we had tried to convince each other of our rightness, of the other's implied wrongness.

Over the years Matthew and I had argued about little things— the safety of microwaves, and whether eating organic fruits and vegetables was really better for you—and big things: whether we should get married, whether we should break up, and (after we had finally ended our relationship, back when I was twenty-five) whether we should get back together again. This last disagreement endured more years than it should have. Sometimes we had talked about it; other times, I had avoided talking, and in doing so, I must have hurt him more by what I did not say.

If you have ever felt that you are not loved for exactly who you are—by someone who professes to—then that love is the one thing you will seek. After my divorce, I craved it as if my life depended on it. But he must have, too—not after my divorce, but in all the times he had shown up in my life and asked me to try again, long before I married or had even met my ex-husband, in all the times we had both been so young, so free to choose each other.

I remember the time he called to check on me and rescue me from loneliness when I was twenty-seven and living in Oxford. It was the summer he spent just two hours away in his hometown in Indiana, and he felt like a lifeline.

"Come on. We're going dancing," he said when I picked up the phone. A statement, an urging, not a question—so rarely a question from him—something I both loved and resented.

I gave in. It was so easy to give in then. I changed from shorts and t-shirt to blouse and skirt, and when he arrived at my door, I followed him out of my apartment, down the narrow hallway and stairs and out to the parking lot. I got into his car. He could have driven me anywhere that night; I would have gone.

I let the air blow onto my face through the window as he drove, as he stole me from Oxford. How I wanted to be stolen. He steered and gunned the engine toward highway and Cincinnati and city lights, away from small town, small apartment, and what felt like such a small life. I do not remember where exactly we went salsa dancing, but if I close my eyes, I can feel the weight of his hand in mine on the dance floor, and his touch on my back as he led me in turns. I can taste the sweetness of the vanilla frozen yogurt he bought me afterward, something he had done dozens of times when we had been dating and had strolled along the gritty sidewalks on other Ohio summer nights.

I laughed and laughed next to him in the car, and for those hours I forgot everything that hurt in my life. The sadness lifted and floated from my body like a broken spirit only he could command away.

For that evening, I leaned into him. I had always been able to because he exuded confidence—his wiry frame buzzed with energy and can-do attitude. An extrovert, with a near-constant smile on his face, he uplifted me. The summer we had fallen in love, and then that summer when I lived in Oxford, he shone: like a sun, like a full moon, like a star that could lead me home.

Matthew drove me back to Oxford on highways and then two-lanes before finally pulling off South College Avenue and letting the car idle in my parking lot as I got out. I walked to my building's entrance, toward the glass door which led to a dark stairwell and to my apartment where loneliness clung like webs to the corners.

Before I went in, I looked back.

I did not want to go inside, and I did not want him to drive away, but I did not stop him when he did. Instead, I waved good-bye. In all those years before my marriage, I had let him go each time. I had said no until it hurt, until he hurt, until I could not say it anymore. I had said no until the word became a kind of religion I did not question anymore.

And now, after my marriage and its implosion, I wanted to believe in yes so badly I prayed for it.

In late summer—in that time of year in North Carolina when the heat feels more like rage, when stems and leaves go limp in reply —Matthew wrote me a letter, as he sometimes did.

I always loved his script because I knew it so well: small loops in perfectly straight lines across the page, as if he were sewing sentences onto fabric. I could almost feel their softness if I ran my hand across the words.

He started the letter by calling me precious. On page three, Matthew told me my heart was beautiful and that Jesus wanted all of it. "Choosing Him is the most important prayer I have for you," he wrote. "Please commit your heart to Him fully."

He wrote that he knew it would not be easy. "Turning from your past, and breaking from the pressure of family and culture can be difficult." What he meant was I needed to steer away from how my parents—the most generous-hearted people I knew— had raised me religiously, not just in Christianity but with a respect for all world faiths.

On the hardest days, their beliefs, now mine, buoyed me: that everything happens for a reason I might not understand yet; that life is a series of lessons I can get right or repeat; and that kindness and respect matter more than doctrine.

He was asking me, in essence, to take it all back, renounce what I had known, abandon what had come before.

But what I wanted to take back was not my faith, or my God, or my version of Truth. I wanted to take back that night in Oxford—not the whole of it, just the moment when I had pulled at the door handle, stepped outside his car, and moved away from

Matthew and toward the building's entrance. If I could have taken it back, I would have let the car idle with me still in it, let the exhaust drift from the tailpipe like grey plumes into the darkness, let the humidity crawl in through the window and surround us. I would have said to him, "Don't go."

But Oxford lay 534 miles northwest of Chapel Hill. In another state. Six years too late.

And in the end, if I had taken it back, what then? Would that have severed the storms from our story? We might have never saved ourselves from the rest of it. Maybe in Oxford, I had let him drive away because I'd had the kind of faith in myself I thought only other people had in other things. The kind of faith that pushed you past your failures, made you rise up from the pain. The kind of faith that waned and nearly broke in two, but if you kept it, it kept you.

We have not spoken in over a decade, but I remember him. Now, I use the dog umbrella but only during light, un-slanted rains, as it is small. I wear the top with the buttonhole neckline but only when the seasons shift, as it is made for neither hot nor freezing weather.

I still have the ring, though I do not wear it or keep it in my jewelry box. Instead, the ring with the round stone drifts like a vagrant around the bottom of a purse. I move it from handbag to handbag, but without any reason I can find logic in now.

Sometimes many months pass before I happen upon the ring again, and when I do, I am surprised by the little gold band, and how shiny it is, and the smooth stone that looks like a green eye staring up at me from the pit of the purse, and how fine and slight the ring is for how large a promise it once held, how big its memory.

CHAPTER SEVEN

After the Waffle House,
This Apology

We'd done this before: negotiated in silences and over meals neither of us had cooked. It always seemed easier to purchase, to sit in hard booths where we did not belong and tell each other goodbye. Sometimes we offered words, tart and bitter, and sometimes we held tightly to our menus or glanced out the windows. Once, I tried to memorize his face in case it was the last time.

Sometimes darkness obscured truth and facts; sometimes I could not see his hands. Back then they seemed capable of stealing things I had given but taken back.

That one time, it was late at night, and we sat in his truck after our last meal at the Waffle House: runny eggs and pancakes and bits of curled and burnt bacon. Maple syrup swirled with a knife on a messy plate. The truth is I don't remember what we ate, but it's what I imagine, along with the restaurant's yellow-hued light, rendering everything sallow and certain. I can't remember who paid for what, only that in the end, this break, and the one before, and the two after, cost us both.

There is a price to goodbye, and what I only understood better, later, was that there is a greater price to taking it back.

In that truck, I wanted to lurch out the door, not sit with him in the cold on that bench seat. I felt the cab tighten and choke. I did not want to talk about the letter he had written me weeks before, the one where he peeled open my heart like a ripe peach, the sweetness escaping down my arms. I had washed everything away in hissing hot water and let it swish heedlessly down the drain, not because I did not love him but because if I kept him, I also kept the person I had been, the one who did not think I could live without him.

I learned, so much later, there is nothing a person can't live without, only things a person can't live with.

He had come to see me from thirty, sixty, eighty miles away—a distance dislodged from memory. Even then, all I knew with certainty was that his drive home alone would be dark, the way bruises are, but that I would ask him to make it anyway.

I never stopped to ask myself what I robbed him of that night, or the afternoon that came nineteen months later when we sat on a bench at the highest point of a slope, no way but down. The sun failed us in its brightness. He asked me again what was possible between us, and I was atheistic in my belief of second chances. I walked beside him to the very bottom and then stole away, pickpocketing things he'd brought—promises, fidelity, faith—in exchange for second guesses.

I was hungry enough then to hoard things that were not mine. Years later, I was starving. I called him from the cave of my car. I called him from the darkness of my silent apartment. I called him from the road, emptied of a future. I left and came back. It was night again, and he opened the door wide, letting in a sky that could never be large enough to contain our constellation of losses.

We ate at a little Vietnamese place we'd never been to.

We ordered soup we had not made with our own hands.

When we didn't know where to go, we ate standing on a city street that hustled with people sure of their destination. We ate on napkins instead of plates, on things we could throw away. One time —was it the last?—we ate while perched on a second floor balcony, right on the edge, so we could see the distance of the drop below.

All along, we took things from one another, but in the end, I took the most. By then he'd learned what I'd learned: what he could live without, what he could never live with.

What, then, of that Waffle House? Why bring it up now?

I push the plate to him across this page: eggs that won't run, bacon not burnt. I know I stole things I should not have. But it's done.

I make the light hanging down white and bearable. I show him both my hands.

CHAPTER EIGHT

The Dance

On the best nights at the Corinthian night club, I salsa danced with Fernando, a married man from Latin America who never brought his wife. He smiled a lot, gave clear hand signals, and never failed to catch the rhythm. He knew enough of the basic steps and turns—and none of the crazy, too-close-to-the-floor dips—to keep me interested. I had gone to the Corinthian in Cincinnati when a friend and I decided we wanted to learn how to salsa dance. We drove faithfully to Saturday lessons, and I became better, but my friend became better still. She dated a salsa instructor from Israel who taught her how to really move, except he only wanted to marry a nice Jewish girl, which my friend was not.

But what did we care what anyone wanted? We were young, then, in our twenties and barely out of graduate school. In that club, what we did was dance. We didn't think of futures and compromises, of mortgages and picket fences, or of jobs we didn't have the freedom to leave if we wanted. We didn't wear coats to the club, even if it was cold, and on that dance floor, we wore beautiful shoes even if they hurt, and always, when we danced, we let the rhythm of the music smooth out our worries. Dancing became a sort of amnesia, and I became separated from the self which brought me there in the first place. I didn't think about the boss who piled work on me, the ex-boyfriend I had given up and later missed, or the man I liked whose smooth face could rumple into anger when I least expected it, which was often. In that space and in that club, I let dance serve as a refuge, a place where trombones, bass, and bongos beat out what clamored to keep me still.

Later, I fell in love with Rob at the Corinthian, lulled by its soft lights that muted flaws and warmed the space between us. We surrendered into each other's arms the first night we danced as if we were meant to be and didn't loosen our hold for the entire courtship. We practiced turns, copas, and cross body leads until they felt like home.

After marrying and moving to Chapel Hill, Rob and I found a bar in Durham, the next town over, where we could salsa. We didn't suddenly give up dancing. Instead we did it bit by bit without knowing we were as we sat more and more often in a booth in the darkness and watched other couples writhe and spin and sway on a floor bathed in amber. The booth's vinyl stuck to our legs, and the smell of smoke clung to our hair as we argued under our breaths about how I wanted to dance more than he did but he didn't like my dancing with strangers, and how the steps we practiced now bored him and he wanted something new.

Three years later, this argument—not about salsa but about everything else—would shout our marriage to its end, and when it did, I wept off pounds of grief and started contra dancing.

The first time I went contra dancing, I wore the exact wrong outfit: jeans and a long-sleeved shirt. Everyone else wore baggy shorts, loose t-shirts, flowing skirts—items meant to keep you cool, to make you feel free. Within a few songs, the back of my shirt clung to my skin, and my forehead and temples were damp and then dripping. But I didn't stop. It was the first time I laughed so hard at how poorly I could execute something. That seemed promising enough.

Once I really started contra dancing, I got the full-blown, can't-get-enough-of-it bug: I found every dance within an eighty-mile radius and showed up, usually with a carload of good friends I'd met through dance, a bottle of water, and a bag of trail mix to share on the ride home. We danced in theaters, old schoolhouses, big gymnasiums, and little churches. I bought a purple backpack for my dance supplies: hair bands, barrettes, hand sanitizer, a spare granola bar, Band-Aids, safety pins, a bag of socks, and most importantly, my dance shoes. The first pair I ever owned were black, soft-soled jazz shoes. One time, I danced in them for seventeen hours during one lovely, thrilling weekend.

I plunged into contra because it's the most forgiving dance. It requires no creativity or innate grace; you follow the caller and can walk the entire song without any fancy footwork. I reveled in its freedoms: change partners every song; lock eyes to stave off dizziness. I could feel a man's arms around me without intimacy; I could feel momentary connection without the heavy emotion of a real relationship. I forgot the distress that hunched my shoulders and the sadness that had plunged into my belly. I started on the wrong foot and stuck out the wrong hand, but for once I didn't lacerate myself over errors. Moving mattered more than mistakes.

You could tell a lot about a man by the way he contra danced. If he pulled you nose-to-nose into a swing and stared unblinking into your eyes, he was intense and flirty off the dance floor, too. If he cranked you in twirls—his hand clutching yours so hard you couldn't help but be propelled in circles—he was overbearing and cocky most if not all of the time. If he gave you no weight on your back when he held you, so that if you leaned away you'd fall, he was afraid in relationships—at best, timid. If he flailed on the dance floor, wild and unaware of boundaries, he flailed while dating you; he cared little about your space or needs.

These rules broke now and again, but mostly didn't, at least not at the Carrboro Century Center where I danced. No one told me this. I dated a cranker. I dated a flailer. No one told me, either, that dating in the dance community is only a good idea until the relationship ends. I wasn't in love with the first man who broke it off with me to date another dancer, but I curled up in bed and cried as if I were. I gave up contra for three weeks until it became bearable to see the two of them enter the hall together, so close that their backpacks bumped and their water bottles collided.

I had salsa danced just a few times post-divorce but gave it up for contra. It took me a long time—years, actually—to regularly return to the Latin rhythms I once loved. My friend, Richard, a dance instructor who wanted to learn salsa well enough to teach it, recruited me to practice with him. Once a week, we crammed into his little home office and watched video clips of a man in tight black pants doing salsa moves with an array of female dancers in high heels and skirts the size of handkerchiefs. Richard scribbled notes; I tried to memorize. Then we would emerge and step onto the honey-colored hardwood floor in his living room, furniture shoved to the sides. He would go to the stereo, push play, rush back and stand straight, chin up, head high, and wait for the horns to blare.

With a gentle tap here, a slight touch there, Richard led me through side steps and twirls, and it was all fine until I anticipated the next move, which I was prone to do. Richard reattempted the lead; I jerked in the opposite direction. He pushed harder; my hand resisted in a clench, my arm stiffened, not because I didn't want to go that way but because in my head it wasn't the right way. Richard let out a sigh that sounded more like a curse of air, dropped his hands from mine, and marched to the stereo. He jabbed the stop button and turned to me. Maybe if I'd been wearing five-inch heels and a tiny skirt I would have had the panache to blame him instead, but I stood there in jeans and jazz shoes, and we both knew.

It occurred to me one night—as I drove from Richard's house in Durham to my place in Chapel Hill, as I pulled into my parking lot, clicked off the engine, and regarded the dark and lifeless windows of my condo—that maybe not knowing what's to come is better. Maybe the nexus of my heartbreaks was an unwillingness to trust life when it veered from my expectations. I always ached for whatever got lost in the swerving.

The next time we danced, I let Richard lead.

And the next time a man I was seeing told me he would rather spend his Saturday evening working than spend it with me, I didn't weep the way I had before. That night, hours after the winter sky darkened, I did the thing I had taught myself to do post-divorce: I went dancing by myself. I put on a black dress, grabbed my dance shoes, and drove to a little dance studio twenty miles away. A string of white lights hung high on a mirror-covered wall. A DJ popped in CDs of music—swing, salsa, waltz —and the small crowd shifted and swayed to each new beat. I danced with no one in particular and with anyone who asked, not getting people's names, not getting too close to anyone but enjoying being held, even just for a song.

The time after that, when a man told me, "I think you're more into me than I'm into you," I didn't cry at all.

Instead, I awoke early one morning in the haze of an already hot May day to pack the car with snacks and water bottles and ride with friends to a twelve-hour contra dance in the Carolina mountains. The highway turned from four-lane to two-lane and wound higher until we could see through treetops and catch flashes of sun washing the green valley below.

That day, I met a man on the dance floor with a steady swing and with eyes as blue as a summer lake. When we danced a second and third time, and he told me he was Preston from Tennessee and later asked if I wanted to see him again, I didn't think about the fact that he lived four hours from me, that I didn't want a long-distance relationship, that he might want things out of life that I did not.

Ok, I thought about all those things. But we danced, and I said yes.

CHAPTER NINE

An Unexpected Light

Sometimes I wish we could start over—not so we could change the past, but to live it all again. I would rewind the clock eight years to that Saturday night contra dance, after I had escaped the crowds to cry in the back hallway of the Carrboro Century Center. Tsafi hardly knew me, but she followed me anyway and asked if I was okay. I told her I was just a little blue. She embraced me for a moment but asked no more, and we stood together next to the metal folding chairs, stacked high, as if they could topple at any moment. We heard the caller command a hands four and the fiddler strike his bow to start. Still, Tsafi did not leave, did not rush out to find a straggling partner, did not look away. After I composed myself, we pulled open the heavy double doors and ducked back into the swaying, whirling crowd.

That was the first but not the last time we stood in the back hallway of the Century Center, in that town just outside of Chapel Hill. In other months and other years, we slipped away to talk in our quiet space, the music and chatter muffled. I often stretched there before dancing, and Tsafi kept me company, her presence pushing off the darkness lingering at the hallway's end. With her Israeli accent, Tsafi spoke with a staccatoed pronunciation I never tired of hearing, and she often gave a little laugh at the end of her sentences. We talked about men we liked and men who got on our nerves—those who pulled us too close during the swing or held our gaze too long. Tsafi could not stand sweaty men with bad breath. I disliked married men who flirted with me as if they were single. We talked about couples who could not keep their hands off each other, and about those who had broken up, who showed up separately, who danced in different lines. And when the breakup was some man and me, Tsafi remained at my side before and after each set in the dance hall. If we ended up in separate lines, we searched for each other, standing on tiptoe to peer over other heads—men with tie-dyed bandanas, women with pigtails or braids—as if keeping each other in our sightline would somehow stave off the pain.

What did we know then, back at our beginning, of endings, of goodbyes?

I still picture Tsafi with the long and yellow hair she had when I first met her and until she lost it, years later, to chemotherapy. Her hair was one of the hardest things for her to lose. Even when she carried more weight than she wanted, her solace was always her beautiful cascade of blonde hair. And because she worked at a salon, first-time clients checked out Tsafi's own style, color, and cut to assess her skills before they relaxed in her chair. What would it mean to have no hair?

Once her chemotherapy started, she did not let her hair disappear in chunks, leaving empty patches. At the earliest sign it was falling out, she shaved it all off. Immediately after, she wrote this in an email: "Turns out that my head is perfectly round and I look like a little monk."

Her hair grew back for over a year, and though she kept it cropped and short, that was never how I imagined her when we talked on the phone. I pictured her the way she was in the photo in my living room—before her cancer. She was fifty then, and her blonde hair and easy, unabashed smile reminded me of summer, a season so long with light it felt like it would never end. The photo was taken on the day I married Preston, several years ago, just before I moved to Tennessee from North Carolina. Tsafi's hair was parted in the middle, and it flowed onto her shoulders in waves and settled onto the white lace of her blouse. My arm was around her, and my right hand was touching the ends of her hair so that a thin strand—of what she would lose later but had not yet —was caught in my fingertips.

Preston and I ended up together in large part because of Tsafi, who had twelve more years of wisdom than I did. When Preston and I had just started dating, I began anticipating why we would not work. This is what a person does who abhors loss, who is in her late thirties and divorced, who wants to suss out any barbed truth before getting tangled in it.

First, it was that he lived too far—four hours away, in Tennessee—from Chapel Hill. "I don't do well in long-distance relationships," I said.

"Just see what happens," Tsafi told me. "Be open."

Then it was: "He'll want children, and I don't want them." I had decided in my twenties that raising children was a weight too heavy for me to bear, that too many things could go wrong, could flail out of my control. "What are the chances he won't want children? Every guy seems to want children." I was good at having conversations with myself, a morose account of how things would break and crumble. "I need to ask him about this. Might as well bring it up now before we go any further."

"Stop it," Tsafi interrupted. "Are you going to end this relationship before it's really begun?"

"Well, it's more that—"

"You're not going to ask him anything about kids right now."

"But Tsafi—"

"No. You need to just get to know each other right now, let yourself see what is possible. That's it. Do not bring up children unless he asks you about it. *Just be* for a while."

To just be still challenges me. I am a person who likes to prepare for what will happen, but few bad things occur with ample notice. And even if there is notice, I tend to miss it, can only see it fully looking back, realizing in retrospect maybe the large-screen television Rob wanted so badly wasn't because he loved cable but because he wanted to avoid me.

The entire time I was married to Rob I fretted over the idea that he would die and leave me alone. It did not occur to me there are other ways to leave, or that I could survive it if he did.

In 2001, just after Rob had told me he wanted a divorce, on one of those December mornings when I was back in Yellow Springs in the company of my parents to try and cure the ills of grief, my mother and I watched an interview with the wife of Tom Beamer, the man who said, "Let's roll," and helped lead the rebellion on that fated September 11 flight that crashed in Pennsylvania.

After Beamer's wife recounted the story and described her loss, I said to my mother, "My goodness. I can't even imagine her pain. I would hate to lose my husband."

And my mother turned to me and said, not unkindly, "You did."

Tsafi almost decided against chemotherapy. "I mean, everybody dies," she said to me over the phone. "It's just a matter of when." But as much as Tsafi thought she could become ready, her daughter—in her mid-twenties and single—could not.

I drove to Chapel Hill and visited Tsafi in the middle of her months of treatment. She had asked me to meet her in the parking lot of the salon where she worked, after her shift. By then, the last fall days had shortened, leaving us little light, and cold.

She hobbled from the bright lobby into the night, across the black pavement to my car and blundered in. She exhaled, and the air steamed into cloud.

"What do you want to do?" I asked after we hugged.

"I don't feel well," she said. She leaned against the headrest and closed her eyes for a moment. "I can't eat, but I am thirsty." Through the windshield, I could see the salon's strip mall cluttered with restaurants, a drugstore, and the big white letters of the Harris Teeter grocery. But Tsafi didn't have the energy to trek the fifty yards to reach the other side, and she would not let me run the errand alone. We drove around the corner to a drive-thru.

She gulped soda through a straw, and with her small hands she clutched the drink container in her lap. We parked again and cranked the heat higher and shifted in our seats so we could see each other. Her face wore the dark lines of circumstances I had not stood beside her to bear: the nausea, the needles in her arm, the liquid in her veins trying to alter the course of her life.

When I was eleven, twelve, and thirteen, I had a friend named Cecily. We were the kind of friends who spent the night at each other's houses, who passed notes—folded into intricate shapes—back and forth in class, and who often liked the same boys and giggled about them. But at the start of high school, we drifted apart, and by the time we were juniors and she sat unbelted in the back seat of a friend's car as it swerved out of control on Route 68, by the time she slid out the door and into the warm breath of a late spring night, we were closer to acquaintances, and then she was memory.

Cecily was the first person I knew well whom I saw lying in a casket. I was seventeen. The freckles across her face were buried and nearly forgotten under a layer of powder and rouge.

Through the whisperings of our small village, I heard that in the weeks before her death, she had gathered back the things she had leant her friends—her red high tops, maybe, or her UB40 cassette, her gold hoop earrings—as if her body and spirit knew this accident was racing toward her. Did she know? Did she guess?

Will I know?

When Tsafi's treatment ended, the scans shone clear, but after a few months, new scans showed that the disease persisted. She had to make a choice. Though only fifty-five, she decided not to undergo the slow poison of chemo trickling into her body again.

I visited Tsafi just after she found out the cancer had returned. We sat on two metal stools in a crowded Whole Foods café and leaned in close to block out the customers around us, searching for privacy in an impossible place.

"I don't want my daughter to lose her mother so young" was what she said. Tsafi's legs dangled, barely touching the metal bar where she might have rested her feet.

"I know," I said, though I did not know—I had no children. But I tried to imagine it as I watched my friend hunched in her seat.

Her eyes were rounded with shock. She stared at her food, poked it with a fork but did not eat. She finally said, "I can face this."

It was March, and the wind blustered into the store through the automatic doors every time someone came or left. We did not take off our coats.

Cecily's death told me a thing I had not known: I could lose someone before my life felt meant to. The year Cecily died, my Great Aunt Eloise grew very frail. My father's mother had died before I was born, so we had driven every year or two from Ohio to see her sister Eloise, my father's aunt, in Vicksburg, Mississippi.

Aunt Eloise had divorced her navy sailor husband after a brief marriage and never had children. She had worked as a civil servant in Occupied Japan just after the Second World War, and then in West Germany, where she started collecting vintage furniture before returning home to Mississippi. Alone, Aunt Eloise rattled around in and sold antiques out of a house so haunted she had called the police on nights she heard the clatter of what she assumed were people breaking in and shoving boxes across the floor. The police never found anyone, and Aunt Eloise eventually shrugged off the noise. She was a voracious reader, cigarette smoker, white bread eater, and Coke drinker. And boy could she talk: you would find my father in the kitchen and hear Aunt Eloise in the living room, chattering away, and ask him, "Who is she talking to?" and he would say, "Me."

The spring Cecily died, Aunt Eloise's prattling also ceased, and every story I might have heard—had I listened when it mattered—got swallowed up into a lonely, hollow silence.

I lost my mother's mother, my *abuelita*, a year after losing Aunt Eloise. I was eighteen by then and about to leave for college. I was never close to my *abuelita* since I lived in Ohio and was a bubblegum-chewing, sneaker-wearing, boy-crazy American girl, and she was six decades older, spoke little English, and lived in a pastel house on a Mexico City street. I knew things about her, mostly from my mother and *tías*: that she had a twin who died at birth; that before she married my grandfather, an American had loved her, and she, him; that having endured the effects of the Great Depression, she could not throw out anything, not even a single dinged-up pot. As a child, I had refused to learn Spanish, so only in eighth grade did I begin classes to learn a language I am ashamed now I did not know earlier. By the time I was sixteen and seventeen, I understood some Spanish but never enough to catch up in closeness to what my *abuelita* and I might have shared had I spoken with her all along.

Only many years after her death, and Aunt Eloise's death, did I realize I could lose a person before I had the chance to ask her all the things I would want to know.

Tsafi was the friend to whom I confessed things I did not want to confess to myself, such as the moments when, despite my being in my forties, I was jealous of my sister for getting more of my parents' attention, or the times when I made a petty or selfish remark to Preston, the kind I immediately regretted and that made me wince. She was the friend who asked me to read my writing to her over the phone. She told me the truth when I asked how I looked, and she always wanted to hear how I was doing and what I did over the weekend, even though she was dying and whatever I told her could not possibly be as important as what she was facing.

But one day, she did not ask about my weekend. "I'm definitely turning yellow," she said. It was September 22. Since I had moved to Tennessee, she and I had talked weekly, sometimes every few days, but by this point I had not seen Tsafi in six months—since March at the Whole Foods store. Just knowing she was jaundiced made me blanch. The tumors had invaded her liver, leaving little space for time.

Tsafi strained the words "It isn't good" into the phone as soon as I picked up. It was September 26, and she had just finished her appointment with her oncologist. She was sitting in her parked car in the hospital lot, unsure if she could drive home without crying. She told me the doctor did not know if she would survive the eleven and half weeks until her daughter, still single, was to give birth to Tsafi's first grandchild, a boy.

"I didn't want to hear that," she said. She was determined to stay alive for the birth. In the next breath, though, she said the doctor had told her that her three siblings—two in the Middle East and one in South America—needed to start booking flights immediately to come to the States to say goodbye.

She wept into the phone, and I said I was so sorry, and I sat on my bedroom floor holding the receiver. I stared straight ahead, focusing on the white light through my window and the swirls of brown in the rug, trying to remain stone-faced so I could hold it together.

"I'm not afraid of never seeing the trees and butterflies again," she said. But she did not want to leave her daughter at such a vulnerable time, on the cusp of becoming a mother, alone. When the doctors had been sure Tsafi's cancer had returned, and she had decided not to seek treatment, her daughter had not yet been pregnant, or had not realized she was. Would Tsafi have decided differently had she known? I did not ask.

"I'm so sorry" was all I said. Again those words, so small.

At seventeen and eighteen, I did not cry when Aunt Eloise or my *abuelita* died. Their deaths felt far away. I saw neither one in a casket: my father made the trip alone to Aunt Eloise's funeral, and my *abuelita* had no ceremony, no service, no official goodbye. Their deaths turned into great losses, I see now, but had seemed like small losses to a girl who did not see either relative often, who was focused on finishing high school, getting into college, leaving home. Moving out of the shelter of my parents' love seemed the deepest loss back then.

During my first autumn in college, I fell for a man who fell right back for me. A few weeks later, he fell for a friend who lived a few doors down from me in the dormitory. That loss—not that of my great aunt or my *abuelita*—caused tears, diminished appetite, insomnia. All over a boy I realize now I hardly knew. Perhaps it was the first time I saw I could misplace things I felt incapable of surviving without: pride, trust, a heart given freely. In my stumbling, I clung to my family, especially my parents, calling them on their Mexico vacation to whimper long-distance about the breakup, each tear costing more than the weeks-long relationship's value. My mother told me she loved me, and he was not worth the pain. Still, my agony over the breakup propelled me down a darker road: I returned home for the winter holidays with my clothes hanging from my thin frame, and I crumpled into my papasan chair for hours in front of our wood stove, unable to get warm. The flames flickered toward my body, and I pulled the chair closer.

That December, I did what I would then do for decades every Christmas: I lay awake in the bedroom of my youth and asked how many were left. How many Christmases would my parents and sister and I be together? How many before I would lose someone—or worse, everyone?

It is not until now that I realize marrying an undertaker was an odd choice for someone who fears loss. Or maybe the perfect one.

I did not think about Preston's profession much when we started dating. Once we married, I began learning what it meant to usher a family through the first bleak stages of grief. It meant calmness when woken in the middle of the night to pick up the deceased, and steady hands to carry and care for the body of someone's parent, child, beloved friend. It meant helping families navigate not only the maze of death but its legal and funerary companions: obituaries, caskets, urns, vaults, grave liners, death certificates. It meant standing still at the graveside in a best suit, even when the temperatures soared or sank, or a storm sliced open the sky.

I heard Preston talk on the phone to the ones who were left, the survivors. His voice was slow and even. "Don't worry," he would say. "I'll help you figure that out. That's what I'm here for."

Preston and I were walking in the cool morning of autumn. It was September 27, and the dogwood leaves had already started burning red.

So many things I did not want to ask Tsafi but still wanted to know, like if she had made plans for what would happen after she died. "I don't know if she has pre-arranged her funeral," I said to Preston.

"Does she want to be cremated or buried?"

"I assume cremated, but I don't know."

He and I turned west on Woodmont, the way we always did halfway through our walk. We trod the same streets in the same order every morning, taking comfort in our routines, as if they could keep the world steady.

"What happens if she doesn't plan ahead of time?" I asked. "Who makes the decisions?"

He explained how the decisions belonged first to the spouse of the deceased, and then to the children, the parents, the siblings, and then to other family members. This was the order of the list, and the order was to be followed until someone was found, someone alive and not incapacitated, able to make decisions on behalf of the one who had died.

Tsafi had no spouse. "So this will fall on her daughter's shoulders if she does not plan ahead?"

Yes, he said, unless durable power of attorney was given ahead of time to someone else, and the paperwork needed to mention that the power of attorney also covered the disposition of the body.

"So how do I ask her about this? What should I say?"

"Just ask her if she has made arrangements for her care and disposition after she dies."

I tried these words on in my mind. I stopped on our walk, on Lynnwood Drive, in front of the brick ranch houses we always went by, that were a part of the landscape of our lives, as much as the hill from which fog rose on chilly mornings, as much as the mountain ridge jutting like a skyscraper into the sky.

Preston stopped, too. I put my head in my hands, and he put an arm around me and pulled me close.

"I'm sorry," he said, kissing my hair.

This is the thing we don't want to think about: the aftermath. So few people, especially among the young and middle-aged, make plans for the disposition of their body; for the service, if they want one; for the music, readings, and who will give the eulogy; for what funeral home to use; for the cost and who will pay.

I did not think about these things until I married Preston and started hearing stories: the sleeping couple in their fifties who accidentally inhaled carbon monoxide leaking into their home; the angry woman who chased her lover down the highway and lost control of the car with her child, unbelted, in the back seat;

the daughter in her forties who, with no apparent warning, took her own life.

Preston and I have a will that reminds me of a decision tree, its branches reaching unappealing conclusions: if Preston goes before I do, then X; if I go first, then Y; if we go together (car wreck, plane crash, fire), then Z.

Which letter will be our story's end? Which branch will bend and then break?

One of the reasons Preston's profession fits him so well is he does not dwell on what might have been. He is good with the now, whatever it is. When he did not get into his first choice of colleges, he welcomed attending his second. When he was younger, and the weekend schedule of his chosen profession made dating nearly impossible, he did not regret following his grandfather's footsteps into the funeral business. He focused on his job, assumed that romance would come later. When a person dies, Preston accepts this as the reality of today and works with people to move forward within this reality, not the one they wish could have happened. This trait was why he was okay not having children with me when in fact he had wanted them. He gave up that wish to marry me; I gave up the community of friends it took me years to find, and I gave up, too, the possibility of moving back to my home state and instead moved to his city, not just for a few years but permanently. We each set aside part of our vision of the future because being together was more important. But I am learning from him not to look back. I am a person who mourns what might have been, holds onto it, makes it more painful than it needs to be.

When I ask him if married life has turned out the way he thought it would, he always says, "I didn't know what it'd be like. I didn't think about it."

I, on the other hand, thought about exactly what my life would be like. When I was eighteen, I expected to be married by twenty-six, to write beautiful novels, to remain in my hometown in Ohio, and to be happy—this last thing, most of all, I assumed, as if happiness were a human right or at least an inheritance. But from whom?

When I was young and at the beginning, I believed for far too long that nothing difficult would happen to me.

When I was twenty-seven, I found a lump that felt like a bead near my armpit. My mother met me at the doctor's office, and she sat up straight as he rubbed his fingers across the lump, as he pressed his fingers around my breasts before asking me some questions. The only one I remember is the one that mattered most: he asked if a bee had recently stung me. Weeks earlier, a yellow jacket had landed on my bikini top and pierced right through the fabric. The cyst eventually disappeared, but my fingers touched my chest every month, searching for the next knot, which came a few years later, this time in my breast. No sting this time, but fortunately, again, benign. Over the years, cysts inflated and then flattened. Each one swelled with my worry. I prayed for them to be nothing, but they always felt like everything.

In early October, I drove to see Tsafi. Despite being fall, North Carolina was particularly warm—mid-eighties—so I packed Bermuda shorts for the trip instead of the jeans I had dug out weeks earlier during chillier Tennessee weather.

In the early afternoon, when I arrived at Tsafi's apartment complex, I climbed the stairs to her door, which was wide open to let in the light and so that she could see the pansies she had planted in a barrel pot on the landing.

She had warned me so many times how yellow she was, so I teased her through the open door, "Where is my buttercup?"

She laughed and pushed herself up from her chair, slowly, shuffling toward me as I strode to her and put my arms around her. She was much shorter than I was, only coming up to my shoulder. She was the frailest I had ever seen her. "You don't look that yellow to me," I said.

"Come on out here," she said, and I followed her to her little balcony. Outside, her skin darkened to a greenish-yellow, and the whites of her eyes were tinged with gold.

"Okay, yeah, you're yellow."

I followed her back inside, and she sank into the waiting recliner.

Tsafi spent most of the afternoon lying on her couch. She said it helped her breathe because something was pressing against her lungs— the tumors, we both guessed, were bumping up against everything. Her belly had bulged. Touching it was like touching stone.

While she stretched out, I lay on the floor a few feet away. We mostly talked and flipped through old photos, and I made her a sandwich and helped her take the right medicine at the right time.

In the early evening, we strolled around the parking lot so she could get some fresh air, and we talked about the afterlife. I said, "I want you to tell me you're still there, if you're able to." What I meant by "there" was somewhere, even if not exactly where I was. I knew I would want her to signal to me that she still existed. She promised she would.

Tsafi walked slowly, and though I typically hurried, and she typically ambled—I had always needed to decelerate to not outpace her—we settled into a plod unlike any we had known before.

"But I want something definite," I said. "I don't want to hear or see something and wonder if that was you."

She laughed. "Sure."

We had had this conversation many times before but never made a plan. We tried to make one as the hours waned.

"Well, what's the first thing you think of when you think of me?" she asked.

"Light," I said without hesitation. Tsafi loved a bright day, a sky stretching wide.

We decided she would turn on my office lamp, the one on my desk with a pink shade and a clear finial shaped like a giant marble. We laughed at our scheme, realizing its silliness. Or at least I did, but I wanted her to try anyway. I wanted to believe I could not lose her so completely. We passed the complex's empty pool. As we approached her apartment, we stepped off the sidewalk and onto the road.

"You know what I love?" she said. "It's something most people don't even notice." She pointed to the road. "The sparkle in the pavement."

Then I glimpsed it, a glint of silver in the asphalt here and there, something I had not noticed but now I see all the time, everywhere.

When Tsafi was too tired for lengthy conversations, we clicked on the television and avoided news of the government shutdown by watching an HGTV program of a young couple rehabilitating an old house. During the commercials we critiqued whether they had made the right decision in buying the house and whether their relationship seemed strong and stable. We had always done this—analyzed relationships, mostly ones in our own lives—but since I was married and she was no longer dating, this couple's relationship would have to do.

We could not halt it: the evening reached its final hours.

Tsafi sat up on one end of the couch, and I moved from the floor and sank into the couch's opposite end.

"Are we going to see each other again?" she asked.

"Yes, of course," I said. Then I thought, *are we?* "I assume we will." I reached over and took her hand. I knew it was our end.

"I don't need you to see me right before I die," she said. "I'm glad you saw me like this, in case this is the last time. We don't have to plan anything right now. If we do see each other, we do. If we don't, we don't."

"Okay," I nodded.

We did not turn from each other.

"Is there any last thing I can do for you?" I asked.

Tsafi looked at me the way she had done at contra dances when I had stood on tiptoe, scanned the crowd of dancers for the face I knew, and found her in another line.

Her small hand squeezed mine: "Don't let fear get in your way."

Then we said our goodbye the only way we knew how to: without saying it. Tsafi handed me her camera phone, and I held it out in front of us. She fussed with my hair without my asking before finally facing forward, putting her hand to her chest.

We leaned in close, and I pressed the button once and then let go.

CHAPTER TEN

The Walk Home

It wasn't an emergency, but one morning when I still lived in Chapel Hill, after a particularly heavy snow, I had to go to the hospital for a medical appointment, the kind not easily missed and rescheduled. My friend offered to drive me in his four-wheel-drive behemoth, which I gratefully accepted. I told him I would walk the way home.

It wasn't too far, just four miles, and I had good boots, a warm coat, and a love of the outdoors. After the appointment, I emerged from the hospital worried and fearful—not because of something said in that one appointment but because of all the trips I'd had to make there, the heavy glass doors I'd had to push, the elevator that rode up slowly, the long hallway of doors that all looked the same. And because of all the rest: the fear of trouble happening, a kind of fear that emerges when a doctor tells you that you are at a higher risk for something you don't want to have. I was lucky because I didn't have that something, but I remember that on that snowy day I worried that one day I would.

Then I walked.

I walked on the main road, out of the hospital's reach, and past the university buildings and downtown with its brick fronts and boutiques, though that day the town lay quiet, asleep in the snow. I walked and I breathed and I saw the white on the roofs and driveways and trees. The branches bent down under the weight of the snow. I felt the chill in my lungs, which I liked, which I craved. It reminded me of the place I was from, the cold that had made me who I was. I trudged past people's homes, their histories hidden behind doors and shutters, some of their stories easier than mine but others so much harder than I would ever know. I walked past covered cars and blankets of lawns, past forks in the road and stoplights and stop signs.

I could look back or look forward. I could remain or I could walk.

So I walked and I walked, even after I turned the key and pushed open my front door, I walked on the day after, and the next and the next.

CHAPTER ELEVEN

The Futon

I did not think about how long the futon would last or whether it could endure one move or many, for back then I had no idea of my future. I was twenty-four, and the futon was the first piece of furniture I ever purchased. It was September, and I had just graduated with a master's degree from Ohio State. The room I was renting was tucked into the side of a Foursquare house on Columbus's 19th Avenue, in the middle of several blocks of students' houses, blocks where rusty bicycles leaned against walls, beer cans crumpled on front porches, and the occasional shattered glass glistened in the cracked street.

The futon frame, made of thick and enduring oak, supported a ten-inch mattress so heavy and dense I could not lift it or the frame on my own. I could have bought a single bed, but I chose a double because I was seeing Matthew then, and he often spent the night with me. He was why I had remained in Columbus after graduation, why I had taken full-time work at an insurance company in a skyscraper so tall it seemed as if it could shoulder clouds.

On that sturdy futon on all the frigid nights of late Ohio autumn, I fell asleep tucked into the crook of Matthew's arm and slept deeper than I would in later years. I slumbered entwined with him from darkness until the milky morning light.

That December I bought a Queen Anne style plant stand with cabriole legs that curved one way and then switched and curved another. The stand was veneer, which meant it only looked expensive, its worth much lower than what I thought at first glance. I received a marked discount from the retail price, as I bought the stand from the Bombay Company where I had taken a second job for the Christmas season, out of desperation, really, out of wanting to be doing something besides waiting around for Matthew to finish his studies for the day. He would call at ten or eleven and ask if I wanted him to come over and spend the night on my futon, in the small room tucked in the side of the house.

He had blanched when I told him I was taking a second job. "When are you going to have time for me?"

I reminded him how often he worked, and he fell silent.

White lights warmed the Bombay Company, a store filled with dark furniture, large gold-framed mirrors, and fake floral arrangements. Customers exhausted me but kept me moving. I wanted that most of all. I made my plan to go to Mexico, and

before I left, at the end of that December, I lugged the futon with
its navy blue cover back to Yellow Springs, back into the house I
had left six years earlier, back in through the tiled dining room
and the green-carpeted den and into the white bedroom of my
youth. I must have taken the plant stand, too, but it is lost from
memory. The futon is all that remains. Matthew helped me move
back home, and we shoved the futon frame against the southern
wall, against other furniture that had lived in that room since I'd
left: my old twin bed, the scratched wooden nightstand with its
black metal latches, and the desk that had once been my father's—
a door set atop two grey filing cabinets. At the end of that day,
Matthew sprawled across the futon. He had begun to feel ill, and
he flung one arm over his head and closed his eyes for a few
minutes before he made the drive back to Columbus, before he
told me goodbye.

After Mexico, I hauled the futon frame from my parents' house
out to the yard, near where my father had once built a swing for
me and my sister (exactly at the spot where years later—though I
did not know it then—I would put on a capped-sleeve wedding
dress and link my arm through my father's and take the steps
toward Rob). I sanded the rough slats of wood and stained the
frame to a golden brown to protect it from whatever I might do to
it later. Oak can handle bumps and knocks, and the scars show
just a little, but more than I wanted.

Then I took the frame and futon to Oxford where they
anchored my second-story, one-bedroom apartment with pop-

corn ceilings, a dimly lit brown kitchen, and northern windows that gave an exquisite view of the parking lot off South College Avenue. The futon served as my couch the eighteen months I lived there. It held my weight when I stretched across it to watch television alone; it lay empty when I left town, which I often did to escape the humming of the refrigerator—sometimes the only sound I heard except my own.

The futon came with me and Rob when we moved to North Carolina. I bought a thick cover that zipped over it to protect it. The cover was a deep, English ivy green that reminded me of Christmas and my mother's holiday aprons. Against our apartment wall, the heavy frame held us up in those first few months as we returned from our temp jobs, adjusted the television's bunny ears, and sank into the futon mattress (we were too poor for cable or too many first-run movies). After we got permanent jobs, we bought a condo across town, and the futon moved yet again. As the months passed and then the years, Rob lay across it often, watching baseball games and old Latino films while I stayed upstairs, reading, writing, existing someplace else. The last memory I have of us on the futon together is on September 11, when we flattened it out and lay side by side for hours watching the towers drop again and again to their knees. We were in counseling then, but on that day, on that futon, our marriage seemed small and easy compared to clouds of black smoke and people touching their way down a lightless stairwell with only their hands to tell them how to survive.

Two and half months later, I sat on that futon and did not rise from it when Rob said he wanted a divorce. I felt stitched to it, bound to an imagined future that had long been losing threads. When Rob moved out a few weeks later, I rearranged the furniture, pushing the oak frame away from the wall where we had placed it. My mother suggested more than once that I might get rid of it, but keeping the futon was never in question. It hunkered down in my living room. It was the weight of my place.

I positioned the futon in the center of the room and faced its bent figure toward the sliding glass doors and deck. I wanted to see outside, to witness the changing seasons, to feel time pulling me forward. I slid the pine table from one wall and pushed it to another, as far from what had been as I could. Still, when I touched the table's smooth surface, I remembered how Rob and I had shopped for it together at the unfinished furniture store. We had lugged it home and then stained the table and four matching chairs on a Saturday, newspapers spread below, each of us taking on half the work, half the squatting and bending to brush the legs and hard-to-reach places. The sharp smell of varnish had clung to the air.

Maybe I should have tossed the futon and the table and the chairs. And the wok he had used to make stir fries for dinner. And the rice maker only he knew how to work. And the dresser where he had kept his hiking socks and shorts and those painter pants I always loved with their loops along the leg seams. But then I would have had to get rid of everything I saw, everything I owned, everything I'd been.

For the next seven years, the futon remained the center of my living room, though so much around it altered. I painted the grey-white walls in that room a cream color that softened the light. A tablecloth covered the pine table. On one wall, I hung a new, round mirror with purple roses made of metal.

My friends piled onto that futon for potlucks, charades, and games of twenty questions, and once for a party where I handed out colored pencils, markers, and tablets of thick paper. Everyone drew mandalas to symbolize their hoped-for futures. Sometimes I found broken ends of pretzels or bits of chips when I flattened open the futon for a friend to spend the night. Pieces of things always lingered in the wrinkles.

On that futon, I was told I was beautiful, I was inspiring, I was loved; I was told I asked too much, I was too selfish, I was too damn sensitive. On that futon, a man rubbed my back as I wept, even though the tears were for someone else; another told me I was the type of person he wanted to marry someday, but he never asked.

On that futon, I meditated, propped myself up with one elbow and watched too much television, and scrawled pages in my journal so I could make sense of the world.

At some point, one of the futon frame slats broke. Too much weight? Too many years? Was the futon finally giving out? But no, it still supported the soon-to-be-ex-boyfriend who slept on it when we argued, which was on countless summer nights.

I am more nostalgic of the futon now that I am writing of it. It held up through fifteen years of my life. Somehow, like a great love, I thought the futon would be mine forever. I am surprised how easily I gave it up. I was getting married to Preston and moving to Tennessee, and I did not want to take the futon. By then, it felt as if it belonged to someone else, or at least no longer belonged to me.

I put an ad on the Internet and waited for a call. Several came, quickly. How much did I ask for? It's a price I can't remember. But I do know a young man showed up and paid in cash. He brought a friend, so I did not have to help him drag the futon across my carpet or bear the heavy mattress and wood frame on my back. I let them shoulder the futon out my front door. I did not watch them drive away.

I thought I would never miss the futon, was so sure it would never miss me. But here I write and wonder: Where is it now, this witness to my history? Is the wood stained a dark and golden brown even now? Is the frame's slat still cracked? Does the green cover carry any scent that's left of me?

CHAPTER TWELVE

How You Know

From the moment I met her, I did not like the little dog. I knew I was supposed to. After all, Preston and I had been waiting for her for months, and we had talked on and on about how much joy she would add to our lives. I wanted to like her, and I had planned to like her. But I did not.

We stood in the parking lot of Mize's Farm and Garden on a cold and dreary Friday, and she glanced up at me with her yellow-brown eyes, sniffed me a few times but moments later caught the scent of something else and wiggled away. She tugged at the leash that Preston held, and as he gripped it to make sure she did not run off, he said, "What do you think?"

He was beaming, and I wanted to say the perfect thing to make my husband of a year and a half happy, but I could think of nothing enthusiastic to say that was truthful. I had half-expected our new pup to come bounding toward me and to instantly fall in love with me—the person who worked at home and who would therefore be the one taking care of her most of the day. But she had not even wagged her tail.

At fourteen weeks old, aside from her white chest and the white tip of her tail, her entire ten-pound body was covered with brown ringlets. Clearly, with her round muzzle and round paws, she looked cuddly the day I met her outside of Mize's, but I can only see that now, through the lens of several years.

She isn't even cute, I thought back then. She was a brown blob and a lot of work, and by the time twenty-four hours rolled around, my feelings had not plateaued: they had intensified. I could not stand her. She whimpered, she whined, she howled and howled when I tried to put her in her crate, she wandered and tugged when I tried to walk her on a leash, and I could not tell when she had to pee, so I took her out every half-hour, but she hated the cold, so she would not do a thing until we got back into the warmth of the house. That's then she squatted, and I groaned.

The only dog I grew up with was Sable. My father bought her without my mother's permission.

"Let's just go look," he said to my mother when he heard a farm was selling Shepherd puppies. "We won't buy."

My mother agreed, not knowing they would return from the farm with Sable curled on my father's lap in the front seat as he drove. Sable was a golden German Shepherd, which meant she had mostly yellow fur without the typical black shades. She was the gentlest of the litter, and my father fell flat for her, as did I. At four years old, I spent my every waking moment with Sable, and I did not understand that canines and humans were two different species: I believed when I grew up, I would be a dog.

Sable and I romped in the snow and in the grass. I leaned on her on long car rides and fell asleep nestled into her fur. I dressed her in scarves and sunglasses, we played hide-and-seek, and I told her my secrets, whispering into her soft ears so no one else could hear. We grew up together, but then, when I was seventeen, Sable's hips gave out, slowly at first, and then suddenly, until the day my father came home from the vet with just a leash, his head bent toward the ground.

After that, I did not pet people's dogs. I did not coo at them, and I certainly did not ooh and aah over puppy pictures. If we passed a dog, I looked the other way. I would remember Sable struggling to get up from the brown pillow she slept on, setting her front legs firmly on the ground, but her back legs quivering. That memory was enough to turn me away for a decade.

Sable's death was a knot in a string of deaths in my life at that time: my Great Aunt Eloise, who was a feminist before there were feminists in Vicksburg, Mississippi, and who was such a voracious reader she once read *Gone with the Wind* cover to cover in one night while sitting on the toilet; my maternal grandmother (and the only grandparent I ever knew) who lived in Mexico and who wore dark scarves to cover her neck wrinkles and who would not smile when she laughed so as not to create lines around her mouth; and the high school classmate who flew out of the back seat of an out-of-control car on Route 68 between Xenia, Ohio, and Yellow Springs because she was not wearing a seatbelt, and because life took things away in instants I did not yet understand.

All those deaths meant more than Sable's death because they were people in my life, but they were less believable because they were sudden: I had not watched any of them crawl to life's tough end. My two relatives lived so many miles away that the news of their passing seemed more like rumor than truth, and my classmate's death I heard of and could picture, but I had not watched her or my great aunt or my grandmother suffer.

Witnessing suffering throttles the heart. If you have never watched something or someone struggle toward death, count yourself lucky.

I did not have another dog in my life until I met Preston's two older Jack Russell terriers, Barney and Boog. As I fell in love with Preston, I also fell for them. By the time I knew them, the stories of them digging their way out of the yard and biting people had morphed into myth. Barney had lost most of his teeth, and since he was nearly deaf, he depended on Boog to alert him to doorbells and visitors. And if Boog had ever loved to take long walks or run, she had lost all that zest by the time I knew her. She was content to loll around on the plush doggie beds I bought for her and Barney.

After Preston and I married and I moved into his house in

Tennessee, the dogs slept near my desk while I worked as a writer from home. I was happy for their quiet, to see their bellies rise and fall in the morning and afternoon sun.

Then one Thanksgiving morning, Preston and I drove with both dogs to meet my family for a few days near West Jefferson, North Carolina, in a cabin in the woods. We did not often take the dogs with us on travels, but Boog had been sick and needed a regimen of medicine I thought might be too demanding for the young boy who usually took care of them when we vacationed. So, at the last minute, Barney and Boog, their beds, bones, food, their leashes and meds, and their little winter jackets got packed along with our things.

But at a gas station toward the end of the two-hour trip, I noticed Barney's skin seemed to be sagging at his throat. Preston noticed, too. We shrugged it off and got back in the car. By the time we arrived that afternoon at the cabin in the woods, Barney's white, furry face had blown up to the size of a small football. We didn't know what was wrong, but we were sure it wasn't good. Barney wasn't just old, but in the months preceding this particular day, he had become increasingly frail and now suffered from dementia. He often walked toward walls and stood facing them for a while before realizing where he was and figuring out that turning around might be a good thing. Barney had been my running buddy, but more recently, he couldn't keep up with even my slow jog.

And so, on that fateful Thanksgiving, as his face grew bigger and bigger, we knew his end was looming. We ate an early and somber

Thanksgiving meal with my family before getting back into the car with Barney and driving through the darkness toward the closest emergency vet in Boone. We talked about Barney on our way there, and though I don't remember now which stories we told, I do know there were plenty: Like the time Preston was sitting with Barney on a lawn for an Alison Krauss concert. Barney was a pup then, still learning the ways of the world, and he must have noticed all the other dogs on the lawn and decided to mark his territory. Except instead of peeing on the grass around where Preston sat, Barney lifted his leg and peed right on Preston's back.

In his old age, Barney had lost many things, including most of his teeth, but he had never lost his Jack Russellness. He still strained at his leash when faced with other barking, snarling dogs, especially the neighbor's that I dubbed "Cujo," who lunged at us and threatened to run through his electric fence every time we walked by. I loved Barney in part for how tough he was, so full of fight, even one he was sure to lose if tested.

But that Thanksgiving, as the headlights of our car cut white into the night, Preston and I were sure his fight was over. By the time we were led into the examination room, we had each held Barney, and we had each cried.

The vet inspected Barney for only a few minutes. Bad news never takes long enough to really be prepared.

The vet looked at us. We braced ourselves. "He has an abscessed tooth," he said, handing us antibiotics. "He'll be fine."

In a moment, Barney was back in my arms, and we were on our way to the car, back to where we'd started.

That night we drove again to the cabin in the woods with our old dog, grateful for time we thought had run out, grateful for a life we weren't ready to give up.

That night, we didn't know yet we only had a few more months. We only knew we had another day, and maybe another, and that suddenly seemed like so very much.

Barney forgot where the doggie door was from the backyard. He wandered and wandered, cutting a path in the grass along the porch, unable to find his way back inside. Winter was coming, and Preston and I took a deep breath and tried to come up with a plan.

That is how the idea of a pup came. At best, a puppy would bring a young energy to Barney and hopefully prod him to move more and play a little. At the very least, the new dog would be a companion to Boog once Barney died. Barney was two years older than Boog, and she had never known a life without him.

The puppy was our way of holding onto the things we could not really keep for long: possibility and hope.

"I don't want a frou-frou dog," Preston said when we talked about the type of dog we wanted. He was sitting at his desk scrolling through lists of breeds on the computer, and I sat on the couch nearby.

"So a Yorkie is out?" I loved the idea of a pint-sized dog I could scoop into my palm. "How about a bichon frisé?" I adored the puff of white fur, and we had decided we wanted a low-shedding dog since Preston had discovered over the years that his eyes watered and itched every time he touched the Jack Russells and then touched his face.

"Small dogs like that are notoriously hard to housebreak," he said.

"Well, I want a dog I can pick up."

This was because of my friend, Scott, and his black lab, Abby. The two of them went hiking one Saturday in Linville Gorge, trotting along the trails together, Abby's tail wagging, until they reached the water below. They rested for a while before beginning their ascent, as Abby was older by then, and Scott, too, needed a break. But soon after they started their return trek, Abby stopped. Her legs wobbled, and she could not make it up. The sun had already begun to slip behind the trees. Scott knew he did not have time to hike back alone and get help, so he did the only thing he could think of: he picked up Abby and carried her miles, uphill, back to his truck.

"How about twenty-five pounds?" Preston asked.

I thought for a few moments. Could I carry a twenty-five-pound dog out of the forest? It would not be simple, but it was possible—much more so than an eighty-pound dog. "I think so."

That is how we settled on an Italian water dog.

The Italian water dog, or *Lagotto Romagnolo*, is on the stocky side, sturdy and strong, now bred for hunting truffles and classified as a working dog. Although we had no work for a dog to do, Preston and I liked to hike, and we took walks every morning, so we wanted a dog who would fit our semi-athletic lifestyle. *Lagottos* are *not* frou-frou lap dogs. They are active, energetic, and too smart for their own good sometimes (or rather for our own good, I now know: able to dig holes at lightning speed in the backyard even as you stand on the porch and bellow a command the dog knows well—say, for example, "Noooooo!").

The breed is also known to be good with families, and though Preston and I have no children, Preston wanted a dog who could be a therapy dog, trained to comfort people in hospitals, retirement homes, and, in our case, the funeral home that Preston owned and managed.

But the puppy, whom we named Kibbi, was not great with anyone when we got her. When people first saw her and said, "Oh, how darling!" and bent down to pet her, she flinched, shrank down, and urinated, to my great annoyance. When we took her to our veterinarian that first day, and she saw how scared Kibbi was of everyone, the vet told us, "You'd better socialize her really well, really fast. If you don't, she'll become a fear biter."

Great. A fear biter. Just what I needed.

I had no idea how to train a puppy, much less what to do with one all day. She yowled and meddled and whined and had no clue where to urinate or defecate.

Preston always says he married me because I am warm and kind, but that dog brought out every shadow of my personality, all of my worst traits pushing forward. I lost my patience with her constantly, swatting her on the butt when she sank her teeth into any garments we dropped accidentally on the floor. One morning I left open the cabinet below the kitchen sink, and I walked out of the room for all of ten seconds before coming back to find she had gotten a hold of an S.O.S pad and eaten half of it, its purplish color all around her muzzle. I could yell so loudly that sometimes I even surprised myself with the decibel level and the adrenaline I felt pumping through my body. On my better days, I forced myself to take a few deep breaths before speaking to her, but most days I just shouted when she did things like sprint out the front door when I opened it to grab the mail. Screaming her name is, frankly, puppy training 101 on how not to make the dog want to come back to you. Preston would emerge from the house and call her name, encouragingly, a happy lilt in his voice, and when she turned around to look at him, he commanded her to stay and strode to her, swooping her up, and said, "Good girl! Good girl!" I would grit my teeth and go inside.

For all my less-than-stellar traits coming forward, Preston's best traits shone. He was the one who slept downstairs beside the dog's crate to take her out in the middle of the night to pee. He was the one who scooped her up when he got home and held her against his chest and stroked her back and rubbed her ears. He was the one who constructed a pen for her on the porch so she would have room to play but be contained while I worked in our home office, and he was the one who cleaned up her mess and who enrolled her in puppy classes at PetSmart. I went to the classes, but grudgingly. I sat in them with my arms crossed, letting Preston lead Kibbi in exercises. I glanced at the clock every few minutes and told myself the quicker she got trained, the faster she would be out of the house and out of my hair.

When I talked about Kibbi to my friends—and Preston was out of earshot—I called her the little brown demon.

Six weeks after we got Kibbi, we knew we had to put Barney down. Preston and I had struggled with knowing when the right time was to say goodbye. We had asked our vet for help, and she told us this: write down the five or six things that make Barney's life a good one, and once two or three of those are gone, you know it's time.

The day we knew, Barney's back legs were giving out, and we stood together at the kitchen window, looking out into the yard, and watched Barney—walking fine, stumbling, walking fine, stumbling, in a rhythm that felt like the ticking away of time. He was also losing control of not just his bladder—that had started already and was increasing in frequency—but now his bowels, too.

Because it was a Sunday, Preston and I drove Barney to an emergency vet out by the airport. It was March, when winter should have ceased but had not, when the air still ached with a cold that felt endless.

Barney, with his wanderings and aimlessness, was thankfully unaware of where we were. His only focus—and the only thing that had made him happy the last few weeks of his life—was food, any form of it: pretzels, crackers, chicken pieces, fried eggs, hot dogs. I had packed a Ziploc of his favorite peanut butter biscuits, and I fed them to him, one by one, sitting with him on the vet's linoleum floor until our name was called. I saved one biscuit for the end itself, when the vet pushed the syringe into a tube connected to Barney, the last thing tethering him to me, and Barney, oblivious, chewed and chewed and chewed that biscuit in its entirety and swallowed it before slumping onto the metal table.

Preston let me carry Barney to the car, his body limp and warm.

We did not turn on the radio, as we usually did while driving, the whole way to the pet crematory in Kingsport, or the whole way home.

Barney had never minded (perhaps because he hadn't noticed) Kibbi nipping at him or trotting beside him, but Boog did. She wanted nothing to do with the puppy. If Kibbi crawled into Boog's bed to sleep beside her, Boog jumped away and curled up someplace else.

But it was Boog, not Barney, who was left to live with Kibbi.

So was I.

"I don't love her," I confessed to my friend Katie several months after acquiring the dog. Katie and I were painting pottery at one of those make-your-own earthenware places. "I don't even like her."

"That's okay," she said, brushing a tray with bright colors. "I get it." Katie had two dogs. One had shown up at her house one morning and never left, and another, Tallulah, Katie had adopted from an animal rescue. Tallulah, I knew, had experienced anxiety and separation issues for months whenever Katie left the house, and Katie had hired a trainer to help her deal with it. But I knew Katie loved both her dogs now, and I wanted to be as patient and loving as she.

"Really?" I stopped painting. "You don't think I'm a horrible person?"

"Nah," she said, still focused on her tray. "When I first got Tallulah, I used to throw the ball for her behind my house. There are woods back there, you know. And I'd throw that ball as hard as I could toward the woods, hoping she'd suddenly dart off into the trees." She stopped painting to smile at me. "I figured if she'd run off, I wouldn't be to blame. But of course she never did." Katie rolled her eyes. "She always brought that ball right back."

I laughed, and we both began painting again.

"Don't worry," she said. "It's gonna be okay."

Here's a list of things Kibbi massacred by chewing: tomato stakes, a plastic bucket, two dog bowls and one dog bed, lots of fencing, plastic bags, a garden hose, the doggie door, a wooden foot roller, cardboard boxes, wastebaskets filled with trash, white office paper, pieces of mail, two stuffed animals (hers, not ours), tennis balls, and too many of Preston's black work socks that she pulled off the clothes dryer and dragged into another room (Preston shrugged, "I can just get more.").

As the months wore on, Preston remained the unfazed owner in contrast to my frazzled self. This is a man who dealt with death all day as a funeral director, a job that required persistent calm as people stormed through grief. Nothing rattled him, not even the things Kibbi had done wrong that I listed off each day when he walked in the door from work.

"You need to focus on the positive," he said.

"What positive? She yelped and barked all day."

"She didn't dig out of the fence. She didn't bite anyone. She's a great puppy—Barney and Boog weren't nearly as good when they were pups."

"But they were great when I met them."

"They were old."

I could not argue with that fact. "Well, I don't want a puppy."

"She'll get easier. This is just a phase."

"What if I never love her?"

"You'll love her," he said.

"When?"

"One day."

"How do you know?"

"Believe me, I know."

"But how? How can you be so sure?"

He laughed and shook his head. "Because I know you."

For the record, I did not neglect Kibbi. I knew the difference between disliking something and not taking responsibility for a decision I had made, for something I had gotten myself into, even if I wanted out. I made sure she had water and warmth, and if we were in a place with other dogs, I did not think twice about protecting her from the aggressive ones—dogs that slobbered and snarled as they yanked away from their owners and toward us. I pulled Kibbi behind me and puffed myself up, making my body appear bigger than it was and deepening my voice before growling, "Back off!"

But I did not pet her. I did not pick her up to cuddle her. I did not think she was adorable, and her yellow-brown eyes glanced at me but never stayed on me. She was aloof to me, at least that is how she is in memory.

She was the first thing I felt forced to love. Or at least expected to. Every other time I had loved someone or something, it had been a choice, and if I did not want to or decided not to in the end, I had always been able to break up or walk away.

But here was this little beast nipping at Boog and scampering around the yard, barking with what seemed like glee, and all I could think was, "She'll probably live at least sixteen years."

The last summer of Boog's life (though at the time I did not know it was her last), Boog and I stole away together. I took a ten-day trip back to Yellow Springs for a writer's workshop, and I packed Boog up with me in the Prius and we sped fast from Tennessee and Preston and Kibbi. During that trip, Boog slept a few feet away from my bed, and sometimes when I read at night before turning off my light, I looked up from my book to check on her, and simultaneously she lifted her head to look at me. We remained that way for a few moments before I resumed reading, and she rested her head back down on her front paws.

Boog's kidneys began to falter the following winter, and Preston and I knew the end was near—so near that as Preston prepared to leave for a two-day business trip, we talked about putting her down when he got back. Preston packed shirts and pants into a carry-on and rolled it down the hallway, and I had a queasy feeling in my stomach as he got into the car for the airport, but I dismissed it.

That night I put Kibbi in her crate and Boog in hers and went upstairs to my room. I fell asleep but for only thirty minutes. I lay there another ten, wide awake, my eyes focusing and acclimating to darkness. No sounds drifted up the stairs, but I had the feeling I needed to check on Boog, so I rose and went to her.

In the forty-five minutes since I had put her in the crate, she had soiled the mat. The pungent smell of urine bit the air. When I opened the door to the crate, she darted out. She had to go again.

There is a cost to loving anyone, or anything. No one tells you that when you are young.

You learn it by what you lose—by the things you must give up in order to keep the thing you love, by what you must relinquish if what or whom you love leaves you.

The other thing no one tells you: that even something small can break your heart if you let it.

That entire night, Boog sprinted out the doggie door and squatted in the yard every thirty minutes, and later every twenty, and then fifteen, before returning to our back porch and plopping down on the softest mat I could find for her. She tried to get comfortable but could not. With her brown eyes, watery and wide, she looked up at me constantly so that I could not turn away.

I sat beside her on the stone floor through that long black night. I murmured to her and stroked her back until her eyelids drooped and lowered for a few minutes. Then out again she would dart and come back in to rest beside me.

I did not leave her, not once, not until I saw the sky shift to grey, to the kind of color that does not tell you whether the day will be bright or dreary, only that it has come.

I waited for Boog to fall asleep again before I pressed my hands against the floor and pushed myself up and walked away from the porch and through our kitchen and into the living room where Kibbi slept. I twisted the latch on her crate and let her loose. Then I leashed her and took her through the front door for a bathroom break outside. She sniffed the air, her nose twitching into morning, before crouching down.

Back in the house, I unleashed Kibbi and shut the door between the living room and kitchen as quietly as I could. I sat down on the edge of our coffee table, bent over, and pressed my face into my palms.

It was just a few seconds before Kibbi approached me. She began to lick my face, her tongue against my tears. Startled, I sat up and stared at her, and she sat down and stared right back at me —for what felt like the first time.

Animals, more so than humans, see you plainly. They do not catch nuances, and they do not believe lies, not even the ones we tell ourselves: that we can lose less if we love less, and that it is best in the end to look away.

I reached down and put my arms around her belly, around her small, brown, and sturdy body—the way I might have done had I been a child, and had she been Sable.

CHAPTER THIRTEEN

Breath and Stars and Time

A round silver pendant, the size of a half-dollar. I wore it on a short silver chain. It must have cost thirty dollars, maybe forty—a price I would never recoup if I sold it to someone else. But I bought this one for keeps. What I mean is I didn't want to ever lose the feeling I had when I bought it—so much like new love, like untarnished hope.

I bought the necklace a few years ago while attending a week-long writing workshop in Yellow Springs. I wanted the pendant to serve as a symbol: of stimulating lectures; of conversations with writer friends in the darkness of Peaches bar, the smell of sticky beer soaked into the floor, our confessions of perfectionism; of long morning walks up Dayton Street for second breakfasts, the way we scribbled sitting at the corners of kitchen tables, shooing talkers away as we hunched over our notebooks.

I wanted to remember how it felt to be a writer and to have ideas shoving their way in the door, toppling over one another, and how it felt to write a sentence laced perfectly with the next. Writing came easy that week the way deep sleep comes easy after a good and hearty meal.

I walked into Ohio Silver and picked out a Celtic knot. The knot is a complete loop, with no beginning, no end. Like a marriage of faith and love, for better or for worse, in sickness and in health.

I have other pendants that remind me of other things: A pearl from my mother-in-law, bought at a local fair, which speaks of her tenderness toward me. A pendant etched in gold I got on the way to somewhere else, a nod to moving on. A blue glass pendant, purchased on a whim, sprinkled with flecks of red and orange, the colors of capriciousness.

I wore the Celtic knot pendant more than any other, nearly every day. Wearing it was as close to a ritual as waking, rising, walking out the door. As close to daily prayer: *please let me be better than the day before.*

I did not think about losing my necklace, just as I did not think about losing my health until I was old enough to feel a knot in my breast. They excised these knots, one after the other in different years, on different doctor's tables, the light harsh, the needle certain. *You are lucky this time* was always the answer. But always the cysts returned like prayer beads hard with uncertainty.

Not long ago I was at a checkup at a clinic far from home. Behind the curtain, I shed my clothes—sweater, shirt, bra. I pulled on a cloth gown, the kind with three arm holes and too many ties, the kind I inevitably put on backwards because there is no telling which way is forward.

Still behind the curtain, I asked the doctor, "Do you want me to take off my necklace?"

"Yes," she answered. "That, too."

I dropped the knot next to my heap of limp clothes.

One year, many years ago, when I could not bear my days, could hardly sleep at night, the year I was certain of something I would not lose but lost anyway, I ran—harder than I have ever run—on winter streets, the trees barren of leaves, my breath smoking in the cold.

That year I listened over and over to mantras meant to calm. The only line I remember now, the only one that mattered then, was: *You are held in the hands of God, and you are safe*. I wanted to stand in God's palm, but all I could think to do was keep on running. So I ran.

Sometimes the doctor's hands are cold. I never care. The search is what matters, whether someone knows what to look for. If you don't know the signs, you will never be certain.

When I am nervous, I do not listen well, do not understand clearly. My armpits tend to smell. When stressed, I don't remember things: I am a sieve that strains out facts, information, reminders. Which is why it was not until long after I had taken off my clothes behind the curtain and later put them back on, and after the doctor had said let's run some more tests in the next couple of months, it wasn't until that night when I was removing my jewelry that I reached to my neck and realized there was nothing there.

There are things you can lose and things you can't. You can lose joy, hope, a sense of peace. You can lose your house and your temper and your pride and all your dreams—watch them lift like balloons drifting into an indigo sky. You can lose your confidence and your keys, friends, jobs, and savings. You can lose your way.

You cannot lose your spirit. It is sewn along your seams. You cannot lose what you do not have. You cannot lose what you do not yet know.

When the clinic opened the next morning, I was standing at the desk, I was repeating: *it's silver, it's round, it's about this big*.

"Do you remember which room you were in?"

I could recall hallways of doors, each one like the next, a row of teeth in a tiger's open mouth.

"Wait," someone else said. "I remember a necklace. Someone found one yesterday when they were cleaning out the patient rooms and brought it to us. The pendant was a tree, right?"

I wanted to believe she had seen it, so I said yes when I meant no. The knot was not a tree. Celtic knots have no beginning and no end. Trees are always moving toward the light, bending toward their end.

In my parents' yard, many summers ago, there stood a young and wispy maple, yearning for sun against an old walnut tree. As the hot humid months bore down on them and on us, we knew we'd have to choose. In the autumn, the walnut tree threw down its green-husked nuts. They plunked to the earth, staining everything they touched.

I was always straining for a kind of permanence. I had a habit of holding onto things, and if left to me, I would have held on until it was too late to save anything.

When the cold began to fog our breath, we took down the old walnut tree so that the maple could lift and flutter its silver-turning leaves.

At the clinic, a department receptionist patted a table in the front area. "The necklace was right here yesterday. Does anyone know what happened to it?" she asked, turning to her co-workers.

"Oh, yeah," said one. "I sent it to the Lost & Found."

Two minutes later, I was there, several floors down. I was saying it again, like a mantra: *it's silver, it's round, it's about this big.*

Yes, I wanted my necklace, but in a clinic if you are one of the ones walking instead of being rolled in a wheelchair, if you are without pain and can walk at a good pace (which I could—I took the stairs my entire visit), if you don't have an oxygen tank, if you are there for a series of checkups and not because you are being treated for an illness or disease, then you should be shouting *hallelujah*. And I was, at least inside. So while I missed my necklace, I was every bit aware that if that was my biggest loss, then lucky, lucky me.

The Lost & Found lady rifled through her drawer of unclaimed items and shook her head. "Nope, it's not here. But it might arrive later." She asked if I could return. I said I could. "Come back at the end of the day. It'll probably be here by then."

I returned at lunch. I returned at the end of the day.

"Maybe try back tomorrow?" she said.

A teacher once gave me this as a writing exercise: *Write down ten things you want stolen from you.* It did not take me long to list off my phobias, though now I cannot recall which I chose—the one of big, dark paintings? Of sharks? Of small underground spaces, of being hemmed in unable to move my arms and legs? Of disease? Of all the things that might be taken away before I am ready to yield them?

Steal any one of those from me.

I've been thinking a lot about life lately. What I mean by lately is my whole adult life and especially in the last few years as I ponder life's purpose and life's gifts. You are luckier the more you look for luck, the more you recognize it in the fabric of your everyday life. It took me far too long to understand this. I've been trying to train myself to notice the small blessings in my days, the quiet but good things I once might have taken for granted, or worse, not noticed at all.

Maybe these are God's universal language.

I went back to the Lost & Found lady only once more—the next morning—before giving up. She assured me the necklace would appear in a day or two, and that she would send it to me.

I went home and waited. I checked the mail every day. A package would arrive, but it would be a book or vitamins or something ordered and wanted, but not the necklace. Finally I told myself it was gone for good. And it was fine, really, in the scheme of things. Such a small thing to lose, almost nothing.

The medical tests would come later: one in several weeks; another, after.

There is a grace in the absence of things, in the still space from one breath to the next when the lungs have pushed out but not yet let in again.

In music, this is called a rest, this interval of silence. I think of waiting in a long line or the quiet at the end of an argument, or the moment just before you know the answer. I think of people standing in an elevator, all eyes turned up, the car going down.

Once, there was a man who came home to his wife, who was standing just inside the door waiting for him, wringing her hands with the dish towel. "What is it?" he asked.

"I have good news and bad news," she said. "Which do you want to hear first?"

"Tell me the good news. Keep the bad to yourself."

She shook her head. "It doesn't work that way. I can't tell you the good without the bad. They're each a part of the other."

He looked into her eyes for just a moment before glancing

down the hall and toward the rest of the house. He slipped a thumb and finger into the knot of his tie and pulled it apart. He stepped away from her and said, "Then don't tell me either."

Is it possible for me to know it all and stand fearlessly in the face of it?

I heard about a woman who prayed that her fear be taken away, and poof, it happened, just like that. Before this act of grace, she could not find peace. Even when the circumstances of her outer life lay placid, the waters of her inner life swelled and crashed, choppy and implacable. She had tried to reach calm seas by rowing in a boat built of virtues, believing that by doing good in the world and paddling harder, she would reach tranquility. Only after her fear had evaporated did she realize that something else (though she could not say what exactly) had precipitated this event. Those former efforts, those struggles, all that expended sweat, had not been what carried her closer to her intended destination.

Great.

Sometimes I wonder if God grows tired of all my questions, all my doubts. *Will I* and *what if* and *how long* and *are you*. I tire of them constantly. Still, I ask.

Perhaps it would be easier if I adhered to a stricter religious doctrine with more rules and restrictions, less forgiveness and more black and white instead of this grey I wade in from more than one faith and practice, a grey muddied and deep that requires balancing with outstretched arms, requires black rubber boots that feel clunky. *I'm more spiritual than religious*, I say.

But perhaps being spiritual is not enough.

You can't pick one thing from this doctrine and another from that one, someone once said to me. *It's not a buffet.*

Yet there is faith in God's silent reminders: The moon spares me when nothing else does. It slits the night open, shows me ground and stone and fallen branch when I have lost my light. It reminds me of a pearl, hard and beautiful, hidden and found, of this, my possibility.

And there is faith in the writing: words are the ladder I climb, the rungs to which I hold. If I keep on writing, the words might also become a net, the kind that catches falling things.

At the clinic, the day I lost the necklace, I turned to gratitude: I said thank you for the foamy latte I drank in the morning, and for the grapes I ate, sweet and plump, and for the sandwich with ribbons of lettuce. I said thank you for all the nurses who smiled and thank you for my husband's presence, how he sat patiently beside me on the bench in the doctor's office and helped me sort one thing from the next. The air was bright and sunny, and I was thankful for that—that I had eyes to see it. This kept fear from creeping in. Until the clinic mistakenly shifted one appointment that messed up the next and it felt too much like dominoes, one clattering down on top of the other.

I stood at the receptionist desk and said *no, you don't understand*, my voice whiny, shrill, and stuffed with tears. I was apologizing to the nurse for the way I sounded even as I was still sounding that same terrible way.

All that gratitude was helping but not solving the problem: which was me.

At that clinic, one of my scheduled appointments was a stress consult. When my doctor wanted to fit in an extra appointment into a day already crammed with appointments, I offered to swap out the stress consult.

"No," my doctor said, without glancing up from her papers. "You should go to that one."

I didn't know what a telomere was, but the stress consultant pointed to her computer screen, to a drawing resembling a shoe string. This is supposed to be a strand of DNA. The telomere is what lies at the end of the DNA strand. The telomere is like a cap at the end of a shoe string, and it protects the chromosome from deterioration. As the telomeres wear away, we age. The more they wear, the more susceptible we are to disease and stress. What makes them wear away? Age. And stress. In other words, we have the ability to slow down the telomeres' decline. In other words I have to worry about my worry causing more damage.

After returning home from the clinic, while waiting for more tests and results, while grappling with my fears of the unknown, I wanted a sign I was not alone, that God remembered this tiny speck of me. This is when I pictured life laughing: *Sign? Sign? But we've already given you so much! Stop asking for more.*

It occurred to me perhaps I was being looked after the entire time, but I was too foolish to recognize it.

The stress consultant had talked about focusing on living in the moment, on gratitude.

There is an art to recognition. It requires practice. And it is true, when I am grateful I stand still in the moment. At the grocery store, I felt grateful I could afford fresh fruits—thin-skinned limes, the scrubbed and red faces of apples. I felt grateful for the trees shifting in the summer air as if they were shrugging off their sleep, grateful for clouds and their wispy beauty. I am grateful for the night sky's wideness and its fever of stars. They make me certain of my smallness.

Which is to say maybe it is better if I matter less than all these bigger things.

Signs come at strange times and appear askew. I have asked for signs before but been too specific: *make a butterfly wing its way in front of me in the next twenty-four hours* or *turn on my pink-shaded lamp tomorrow.*

But signs, like life and luck, don't work that way. They can be beckoned, but they come in their own shape, in their own time. And when they do show up, if you are lucky, then you know.

Many years ago, I was dating a man with whom I argued often.

He was a man who was good at fixing things—my door

hinges, or objects such as drawers, engines, brakes, things that could shut or open, stop and start.

We broke up and then got back together, and I wanted to believe we could tinker with the inevitable and make it work like new. I wanted to believe he was that good at fixing, or that I did not need to be fixed.

At the beginning of our second try, I asked God for a sign: *please*, I prayed, *make it clear if this is meant to be*. But there were no glaring lights or strange fortune cookies or messages that showed up in unaddressed envelopes at the door. There were no snowstorms in September. Instead, he and I argued up and down my stairs and kept trying to fix each other. Until one silent morning—the previous night's heated discussion still lingering like smoke—I slipped out of my bed, grateful he was still asleep. I made it all the way down the flight of stairs and then: "Where are you going?" his voice called out, a match newly struck.

"For a walk," I answered. In truth we often walked together. "I thought you were asleep," I said. "Do you want to come with me?" I was still standing at the door, at that threshold where I'd lingered so many times before.

He said he didn't believe I thought he was asleep.

So I left, clicking the door behind me, wondering whether I should have stayed, if I should turn around. As I walked down my street and onto another, I didn't remember I had asked for a sign. But suddenly, he was there in his vehicle, his window rolled down, his face boiling as I had never seen before. He leaned his head out, his engine revving next to me, to tell me—just before his car charged away, his tires spitting up rocks—"You're going to die alone."

It was only a half-hour later, as the rusted-red sun rose higher in the sky, that I began to laugh instead of cry. Signs do that: they make the truth a gavel, a decree that sets you free.

One night, not long ago, I received a written message from the clinic.

I am lucky to have good health care, lucky to have health care at all. Still, it always makes me nervous to hear from the clinic, so I opened the message with some trepidation. It was the results from the first test, yielding information—not good, not bad. Just neutral.

You're fine, I told myself, *just be grateful you're fine*.

The next day, a phone call came in from the clinic, and again I felt that nervousness I get, but a greater surge. I thought of intervals, the still space from one breath to the next, when the lungs have pushed out but not let in again.

In the phone call from the clinic, the voice on the other end was unfamiliar, and the caller—a woman—seemed a little shaky. I was trying to figure out which department she was calling from and if it was about the first test's results or perhaps the unknown second, and I wanted to ask if everything was okay—which really means *is everything okay with me?*—when she said, "Your necklace just showed up," as if it had suddenly decided to wander through the Lost & Found door.

(Can fear be shaken loose, like walnuts from an old walnut tree?)

My heart leapt.

My lungs let in again: breath and stars and time.

I carried them with me long after hanging up, and they pressed into my hand as if they were mine.

My fingers closed around them, in case they might be kept.

CHAPTER FOURTEEN

Luck

I was the only girl in sixth grade who didn't want breasts, yet I was one of the first in my class to grow taller, to begin having my period, to need a bra. I put off the bra as long as I could, until the summer that followed when my mother insisted it was time—that my breasts were growing too big to spurn support and coverage. She took me shopping and bought me a white polyester bra that I wore for the first time underneath a pink polo shirt to a party.

"Does it show?" I kept asking my best friend, Camilla, throughout the evening, turning around so she could assure me that the part of the bra that spanned my back was invisible beneath the shirt, though I am not sure what I would have done had Camilla said *yes, it shows*. There was no way to remedy that, other than take off the bra, something I would not have done. I knew better than to go against my mother's insistence on anything. I followed rules and directions and expectations, but I hated all the change.

That summer between sixth and seventh grade hung suspended between puberty and adulthood, that tenuous and murky place where boys seemed less like pests and more like possibilities, and girls were leaving the world of unawareness and transitioning to hyper-awareness of weight and posture and pimples.

The bra felt strange against my chest and back, and I squirmed when wearing it. "Does it show?" I kept asking Camilla, but really I was asking: *Do I look different than I used to? Am I still who I was a week ago? And who will I be after?*

I wanted to hold on to what was and never move forward. What I must have believed then—but only articulated decades later—was that moving forward meant losing things. I never imagined the possibility that I might gain things instead.

Today Preston is ironing the back and collar of a striped, button-down shirt. I don't know why the shirt is so wrinkled. I don't ask him how much time has passed since it was last worn or for what other occasions it was meant—he will not know anyway. The shirt is not my husband's, but he irons it more carefully than he does his own. This shirt with its long sleeves must appear perfectly pressed today, respectful, worthy of a promise not kept. It belongs to the son of a friend. That son died yesterday in the early hours of morning while I was out walking our dog on a blue leash and Preston was at home, preparing to go to work, pulling a dark red tie from the closet, brushing his shoes clean.

Owning a funeral home means taking care of the dead along with the ones left: the lost and losing. Preston isn't usually the one who irons shirts for people, but these are the kinds of small things that matter in the face of the terribly big. I am watching him now as he takes out the creases, folds the shirt over, takes out more.

Outside, the sky is marbled white and blue, unable to be just one thing or another. Outside lie our beds of greens, built to hold rows of ruffled kale, spears of spinach, the beginnings of some gold tomato blossoms stretching toward a sun that leaks through the clouds. Outside rise all the flowers I have planted during our young but growing marriage: orange coreopsis, dusky-pink lenten roses, white spirea resembling lace. These plants take their turns opening their petals to the world and then closing.

This is what happened years ago, the summer I was twenty-seven.

"We never go swimming," I complained to the man I was seeing, someone who had started out as my friend and co-worker but had become something else by then. It was a Saturday, and the sound of insects rattled the air. "I've never even used the pool here," I said. I lived in a small, north-facing apartment, and I was always yearning for light.

"Then that's what we'll do today," he said to me.

We found some chaise lounge chairs by the little, square pool, and it finally felt like the kind of summer I had wanted all along instead of the arguments we'd been having about my wanting to spend more time with him on weekends, and his wanting time with me but also wanting his freedom. The sun seemed hot enough to burn off everything that had come before. We splashed around and then stretched out on the chairs until our skin toasted to a darker shade.

"I'm gonna dip in again," I said in the late afternoon, and I lowered myself into the water, my back against the side of the pool. I stretched out my arms and closed my eyes. Then I felt a prick and sting, and I yelped. A yellow jacket darted from my bikini top.

"What is it?" The man I was seeing jumped up and gave me his hand and pulled me out. He rushed back to the chair to grab my towel, and he put it around me and rubbed my back dry. I was crying, and I must have told him through sobs what had happened because in a moment he had gathered our things and led me away from the pool, away from people staring, and he got me up the stairs and into my small and sunless apartment. Once inside, I unclasped my bikini top, and there on my breast a red bump swelled an inch from my nipple. I was still crying and standing, and the man I was seeing—a man who could be both tender and temperamental—left briefly to fumble in the bathroom cabinet and dash to the kitchen. He was breaking up the ice I never used, clunk-clunk-clunk against the counter. Then he was in front of me again, this time with a towel wrapped around chunks of ice.

He was soft-faced, thick-haired, broad-shouldered. His voice was deep and calm enough to steady me in its tone. Everything about him said he was substantial and sturdy, but his face could close unexpectedly, like a moon obscured by a rush of clouds plumed from cold temperatures. One time, he had arrived at a bicycle race frustrated and scowling because he had spent too long searching for me and our friends through the crowds, though I had told him we were standing by the water tower. When he asked if I had been watching for him and I could not say yes—though I knew that was the only right answer—he turned away and ignored me for the rest of the race but talked and laughed with everyone else. He could seal off the world and me in an instant, but in that moment after my sting by the pool, on that late Saturday as we stood together in my apartment, his face lay as open and bare and honest as my chest.

"It's okay," he said, and touched the cold to my breast. The cool soothed with a dull ache. He held the towel to me until I could not feel the pain. He kissed my forehead. He promised not to let go until I was ready.

I was just beginning to understand the edges of how someone or something could both hurt you and help you. It only depended on how you looked at it, when you looked at it, and what truth you decided to see.

About fifteen years ago when I found a lump in my breast, I went to see a specialist, and my ex-husband, Rob—we were then married, of course—went with me. His face lost its color as he waited, silent, seated in the corner of the doctor's office while the doctor pressed his hands into each of my breasts, feeling for the lump I'd reported through tears. Maybe I made Rob go with me. That's more than likely. He wasn't one to want to go to doctor's offices, with or without me. When I had sliced open my thumb while cutting sweet potatoes in the first months of our marriage, it had been a friend who had driven me to the emergency room. Rob had been at work when it had happened, forty minutes away —"You'll bleed too much until I can get there," he had said, and he was right—but I must have stayed out in that waiting room at least that long. I looked for him. I wanted to see him come through the glass doors and find me, sit beside me in the bucket chair too hard to give comfort. Not that he had ever promised anything of the sort; not that I had asked. Both of us were often silent in our longings. Instead, my friend held my hand as the nurse stitched my thumb together. My friend also went with me the one time I had a cyst removed from my shoulder, but that was a regular appointment, not an emergency visit. I can't remember why Rob was not there, only that he wasn't.

After the breast specialist examined my lump, he assured me it was fine, just a benign cyst again, but I had gone through all the terrifying emotions of wondering what it was, reflected in my marriage, which by then was sobering up, all the falling-in-love highs fading away, the reality of our tenuous marriage becoming apparent as our relationship squinted in the light.

A year later, when Rob wavered about whether he wanted in or out of our marriage, I actually gave him a deadline of a few weeks to make a choice. I'm not proud of how I pushed him, but here's what I know about myself, and it was true then and still is today: I can deal better with the known than the unknown. The fact of something is easier than the phantom of it.

My appetite rises and falls in rhythm to my stresses. In my family, we are stress-starvers, meaning when worried or blue, we push away the plate of food, or at best, pick at it. When this happens, we have a term for it: we say, "My stomach has closed."

In the fall semester of my freshman year in college, my weight ran the opposite of others who were putting on pounds due to starchy cafeteria food and too much alcohol. I endured a difficult breakup, and I lost weight. By Thanksgiving, I was thin enough to blow away.

If I am happy, or if I momentarily forget that I should be worried, or if I am eating pho at a Vietnamese restaurant (in which case all bets are off), I eat heartily. But when I am stressed, most foods make me nauseous. When this happens, some foods are more palatable than others. Fruit is easier than, say, meat or bread or milk.

When Rob and I split up fourteen years ago, my stomach closed for a whole two months.

There are people who feed love, and others who starve it. I suppose you can overfeed love, make it bloated and big, saying *I love yous* throughout the day as if the person needed to be reminded. I used to do that. Maybe I still do.

When we were married, Rob told me I needed to say I love you less to him because then it might have more meaning. Perhaps he was right. Or maybe he was trying to tell me to stop saying it altogether.

The truth is that for a long time I believed in something I

did not know I believed in, that was only evident upon reflec-
tion: that love was a currency. If I gave love, I would get it
back. I expected an equal exchange. When I did not feel
enough love, I gave more. (Whatever "enough" is. Back then
it was never enough.)

It was like putting coins in a broken soda machine, banging a
fist on it because it won't drop out a cold can of soda, and then
inserting more and more coins. Not that I am calling Rob a
broken soda machine. My system of love was what was broken.

Most things broken can be fixed. I did not know then that in
the end they might be better with repair.

Some women are in love with their breasts, in particular, their
bigness. My breasts were C cups throughout my teens and twenties, but I do not remember thinking much about their size and
shape other than how many bras I needed (two) to keep them in
place while I ran. The first time I became aware that they might
be considered big enough to take a second glance, I was in
college. A music video company came to campus, offering students the chance to sing and dance to their favorite tunes, all
while being recorded. Two of my friends and I signed up to sing
Grease's "You're the One that I Want," and one of these friends
opted to play some semblance of Danny Zuko while two of us
played fawning girls and paraded around in ridiculous, blue-
sequined, full-length gowns—the only matching costumes the
company had. They were so tight-fitting, we could have passed
for mermaids had the dresses had tails instead of a row of blue

feathers fluttering at the hem. We wriggled into our outfits. We sang. We danced.

Two men recorded the whole thing.

In the video, the camera pans from one person to the next—and sometimes to all three of us at once—but the camera often returns to me, not to my face, but to my chest, my chest, my chest, my breasts moving in rhythm to the music.

I have long had this theory—understood but never spoken aloud to anyone, much less myself—that in order for life to grant me something, I must surrender another thing. A sacrifice is required. It's why I make gestures to God, asking *if I give up this one thing, can I have this other thing in its place*, as if the world remains steady and somehow more fair in this balance of giving and taking, in this sometimes uneven exchange.

This theory is about luck and its limitations. So when life takes away something unexpectedly, if I realize it could be worse, I accept the sacrifice without hesitation. I hand it over and try to step back, turn my head away so I can't be seen, so no one will come to me and ask for more.

Here is a list of procedures I had done to my breasts in a period of thirteen years: mammograms and ultrasound; right breast, incisional biopsy; mammograms and ultrasound; left breast, needle core biopsy; left breast, another needle core biopsy; right breast, excisional biopsy; left breast, excisional biopsy; left breast, ultrasound-guided core biopsy; mammograms and ultrasound; mammograms and ultrasound; mammograms and ultrasound; diagnostic mammogram and ultrasound; right breast, ultrasound-guided core biopsy; right breast, needle-localized excisional biopsy; mammograms and ultrasound; mammograms; mammograms; mammograms; diagnostic mammograms and ultrasound; mammograms; diagnostic mammogram and ultrasound; ultrasound; mammograms, an MRI-guided biopsy and then more mammograms all in a span of two days on one breast, my left.

Over a decade ago, before those first left and right breast excisional biopsies, I asked the surgeon, "How much are you going to take?" He said he wouldn't know how much until just before the actual surgery.

I was lying in pre-op when he came to stand beside me. "How much?" I asked again.

"About the size of a golf ball in each one," he said, kindly but steadily.

Fine, I thought, and I went from a C cup to a B cup bordering on an A cup that day. I no longer needed two bras every time I ran.

Around a decade ago, in the sky of my breast scans a star appeared. Its radiating pattern was what made my radiologist tell me she thought there was a good chance I had breast cancer. I asked what percentage of a chance. She knew me well enough to know I'd rather be told the bare, bald truth.

"Eighty-five percent," she said.

I focused on the fact that I had a fifteen percent chance of having nothing and proceeded with a biopsy, which came back free of cancer.

Eight years ago, I had to have another biopsy, the kind where they put you under anesthesia and someone has to remain in the waiting room, drive you home, and administer pain medication. My parents offered to drive in for it.

"No, they don't have to," Preston said, though we were newly dating and he still lived four hours away from me. "I'll take you."

That biopsy, too, came back cancer free.

I ended up lucky that time, as I had been and would be year after year through other biopsies and mammograms, ultrasounds, MRIs. But that's the thing about luck: you don't know how long it'll stick around.

I suppose that's true of anything, and anyone.

Nine years ago, when I met Preston dancing, I was relieved to discover he was not the type of dance partner who tried kicks and moves too wild for me to understand. His hand was firm on my back, and he did not attempt any dips or unadulterated twirls. During a break, we sat on a bench outside and talked, facing the quiet mountain road as we spoke. The late May air was warm but not hot, neither dry nor humid. We kept on talking as the light rose toward summer. He stayed with me out on the bench even after the music struck up again, notes that could have easily beckoned him away.

Early in our relationship, Preston and I took a trip to Steamboat Springs, Colorado, a state I had never been to before, to hike just before the aspen trees turned gold and marked the coming of autumn. We ate at cafés in town, soaked in the springs, walked in the woods holding hands. One afternoon, back at the condo where we were staying, Preston asked me to rub his back, and within minutes of my doing so, he fell asleep, startling our conversation into silence. I left the room, shut the door, walked up a flight of stairs to another room where he could not hear me, and wept. Fear had crumpled my happiness—fear that I would end up in another relationship that was more give than take. I cried until the sun fell further. Then I got myself together and descended the stairs. A while later, he awoke. I must have been back in the room already, or he must have called me to him because I remember sitting on the edge of the bed as he yawned and sat up. He said, "It's weird. I keep having this nagging feeling that I've done something wrong."

I said nothing.

"Come here," he said, gesturing me closer. "Lie down and let me rub your back for a while."

To want to live a long life is to want to love.

Earlier this year, before the last MRI-guided biopsy of my left breast, the doctors had me wait alone inside a small and spare room to watch a video on how the biopsy was going to work, and I remember thinking, *I just want to get up and walk out of here. Can I do that?*

In the days that preceded the biopsy, as I sat or lay down in doctor's offices while wearing a pair of blue gowns, or as I sat in those same gowns in waiting rooms as HGTV blared in the corner, I had the feeling of wanting to disappear. I did not want to fill out papers—*again?* I thought, *you're asking me these questions again?*—I wanted to not be in doctor's offices period, not have my breasts squeezed between two plates, not get scanned or have to lie face-down and be slid into the bore, the cylindrical opening of the MRI machine, to hear its knock-knocking and buzzing and clanking. The morning of the biopsy, as I sat in that spare room alone, I imagined getting up and going, flying down the hallway in my three-armed, blue gown, white ties like contrails behind me. Everything in my body said, *Run. Now.*

And that's when I thought of Rob.

I thought of how, fourteen years ago, it seemed as if he had high-tailed it out of our marriage, and I thought about how angry I was for so long that he did not want to hang around and fix it. I thought of how frightened he must have felt of whatever tests and trials we needed to endure to stay together, how enormous they must have seemed. Although the day of my biopsy I remained sitting in that small and spare medical office until two attendants came and walked me down the hallway, I finally understood how freeing that decision must have been for him, to simply get up and go.

I used to think our young marriage was simple. Only as the years passed did I come to understand our own complications, how, like cells that have yet to be graded and categorized, we were still without complete understanding, or understanding at all, of what made the other work, of what the other wanted and needed, only that we were failing in our abilities to give each other those things.

Now it's clear. He yearned for a lifetime of adventure and freedom. I yearned for a lifetime of security and love.

If you look for something long enough, you will find it.

I got the call about the diagnosis while Preston and I were traveling, still a few days from home. He pulled the rental car into a parking lot, and we got out and put our arms around each other as the first days of autumn caught up with us. We reminded ourselves that the cancer was early and could be removed. A system broken could be fixed. We could just see the surface of the year that lay ahead, of surgeries and choices, of endings and beginnings, and of the questions I had asked myself in sixth grade that I would ask myself once more.

After the diagnosis, my stomach closed. Preston took me to eat Vietnamese again and again at different restaurants—Pho Chau, Lotus, Quang—even when he tired of it.

But there were other meals, of course. By coincidence or luck, it seemed that a little bowl of fruit accompanied whatever meal Preston ordered—an omelette, a sandwich—no matter the time of day. The bowl of fruit became the perpetual "side" instead of a salad or fries. He did not ask why, nor did I, but there it would appear bearing a couple of pineapple chunks, some melon slices, a twig of grapes.

Sometimes I did not order anything, or I ordered something small and manageable, or I picked at what I had, eating a third of a sandwich before laying my napkin over it as if it had expired.

For each of those meals, Preston, without saying a word, pushed his little bowl of fruit to me.

Without a word, I picked up a spoon, and I ate.

CHAPTER FIFTEEN

Till Divorce Do Us Part

In the weeks after Rob told me he wanted a divorce, I decided I believed two things: First, the institution of marriage was a sham, and I was done with it forever. What was the point of making vows and promises if you weren't going to keep them? And second, that it would have been better facing Rob's death than his decision to leave me. I know that sounds terrible, and it isn't that I wanted him dead *after* the fact. It's that I thought it would have been easier to let him go if I had known he had no choice about the leaving. Easier than hearing he was sure he would be happier without me. Easier than hearing goodbye.

That was nearly fourteen years ago. I was probably standing in the front hallway of our home when I decided those things. Especially in those first few days and weeks, the hardest transition of my day was entering our condo—a space that suddenly felt lifeless and empty. Sometimes after I came in, I sat on the carpeted stairs and stared at the front door, as if I could somehow find a way to go back out, to start all over again.

I got over the first belief—marriage as a bunch of hooey—quickly. I knew I didn't want to get married anytime soon, but I realized (after the initial anger and pain blew away like thick smoke from an unplanned fire) that someday I wanted to try the whole marital thing again. Believing in marriage meant believing I was capable of trusting myself again, capable of love.

But the second belief—death better than divorce—lasted much longer.

I saw Rob twice after he moved out.

The first time was a couple of months later, in the parking lot of a Border's bookstore off 15-501. We agreed to meet there because it was an easy place in between the condo and his rental—an apartment I'd never seen and had no wish to—in a neighboring city. We must have exchanged things although I can't recall what they were. Clothes he'd left? The silverware set we'd split but maybe counted wrong? Mortgage papers? The title transfer to make our old car my new car instead? A check for half our savings, half our joint account, the whole of our marital lives?

What I remember is not what we exchanged but what we didn't: The words I wanted him to say. "I'm having a hard time," or "This hurts." I didn't want him back, but I wanted to know I wasn't the only one suffering. I wanted to know our marriage had meant more to him than something from which to run.

Instead he told me that he felt more like himself than he had in a long time. I asked him what he meant, and he said he could do whatever he wanted, go away whenever he wanted. He was trying to tell me then what he would more plainly tell me later, which was that our marriage had made him feel trapped, that he was not the type of person who needed stability, that he got bored with the status quo. But I was too caught up in wanting what I wanted—for him to be different—to hear his truth. If I had been a better person, I would have felt grateful that the man I had loved felt hope now, and I would have said, "I'm so glad you're happy."

It was dark and cold out. The lights from the Lowe's across the parking lot appeared bright but far away.

When we got to the end of our dwindling conversation, there was an awkward pause as we stood facing each other. We'd always hugged goodbye, but this time neither one of us moved toward the other, and finally I said, "I'll see you later," and I turned and walked away.

The second time I saw Rob, we'd been split up for almost six months. He'd driven over to the condo to drop off or take things. Funny, I can't remember which. He'd borrowed a truck, and I recall something about a lamp, shelves, dishes. I don't know now if the objects were coming or going, only that he was—going, that is, forever. When he finished dropping off or picking up, we stood one last time in our hallway, which was still, at that time, painted a grey-white (I would change it to a spring green a few years later). He was closer to the door. And I did the thing that makes sense now but didn't then (I'd puffed myself up for weeks with pep talks on how I wasn't in love with him anymore): I cried. And it wasn't because I was in love with him—it was because I'd once been, and because he'd once loved me. I couldn't help but still love the idea of the marriage I'd believed in.

"Why are you so upset?" he asked me.

All I could think to say was, "Because this is the last time I'll ever see you."

He looked confused. He didn't think it was goodbye. "Of course we'll see each other again," he said.

And I said to him, "No, we won't."

And I was right. We never did.

Years after my marriage to Rob ended, I read about a couple who kept no secrets from each other. Every thought—however ugly, gross, out of line, or irresponsible—is admitted, confessed, offered up as a way of building trust. Sometimes I wonder what would have happened if Rob and I had told our truths back at the beginning. During those first few months of living in Chapel Hill, I might not have cried while taking showers just so he would not hear my tears. I wanted to be a person who did not lean on my family for security, who was perfectly fine with picking up and moving on. Perhaps he might have said marriage to me, maybe marriage at all, terrified him.

I picture him now in his black wedding tuxedo as he stood beneath the maple tree in all its lush, summer glory. The tree's leaves, fluttering like a great cluster of green wings, cast their shade onto him, but it was useless, for Rob sweated as he stood there, despite the cool day. In the moments before we said our vows, Rob's face was pure white, the kind bleached of all relaxation. He squeezed my hands throughout the ceremony, which I thought meant he was holding on but maybe only meant that he was seeking strength. That night, in bed, he said into the darkness that he was the luckiest man in the world, but perhaps it was said less like truth than an act of faith. Perhaps we both wanted to believe our love was enough to make us each become the person the other wanted.

After we split up, Rob and I each went on, and the pain of our divorce eventually faded. I dated for fun, dated to learn, and dated to grow up. There was so much I did not know. Being married now to an undertaker means that in the years since then I've become a little more acquainted with grief and what it really means to lose someone.

It's only now that I understand that talking with Rob—in the parking lot of Border's, and later in the condo hallway—hard as it was, chipped away at the sadness. Facing him was the first of many steps to moving on.

When I decided long ago that death was better than divorce, I hadn't really considered the alternative. I didn't think about what it'd be like to be a widow. To view a husband in a casket. To find a husband's eyes shut, hands folded but stiff. To see a body but not a spirit. To never know what might have been.

Back then I'd only considered not having someone tell me he no longer loved me. Now that seems easier than the loss of someone who still did.

Though we never saw each other again, Rob and I emailed a few times and wrote one another letters filled with explanations and all the things we had not said. Looking back, I'd like to think that in doing so, we helped each other with the final letting go.

Years after we split, we talked on the phone, once, for a very long time.

Each of us said we were sorry—for different things. But in the end, for it all.

Crossing the Channel

On vacation in the Caribbean, Preston and I ambled into a water gear shop, looking for fins. A skinny young man with tattoos like sleeves told us that, just so we knew, they did kayaking trips. "We're the ones," he told us (describing himself and the two shop owners), "that do the kayaking trips at night using clear-bottomed boats with LED lights." But there were other trips they offered, too, he said, one of which was a venture out to Steven Cay.

"We have to cross a channel on that trip, so we're careful who we take," he said. Then he added, "We don't just let anyone go," meaning it required at least a modicum of physical prowess, and some people weren't up for it.

I should explain that as he told us this, I was standing there wearing a wide-brimmed sunhat, its laces hanging down more like a bonnet's. I confess, too, I had just been asking him about what fins to buy for snorkeling—the long or the really short—and had opted for the really short because I didn't plan to dive. And, to boot, I'd expressed a particular interest in the hot-pink fins.

He must have known what I was thinking because he said quickly, "I'm not talking about you two. We'd definitely take you two." Maybe he said this because Preston was wearing a baseball cap and a sporty shirt and shorts. Not that I wanted to go on the kayaking trip that crossed the channel and went to Steven Cay, but I wanted to be the type they'd allow to go. I told myself he could see that I was athletic, despite the short pink fins and the wide-brimmed hat.

I told myself I was still as strong as I had been twenty years ago. Which maybe I was, but maybe I wasn't.

Maybe it was a different kind of strong.

The first time I ever snorkeled I was in love for not the first time but I thought the last. I was in Mexico with Rob, who had slept in hammocks on beaches and had backpacked his way through little towns where he did not always know the language perfectly but knew how to survive on only a few dollars a day. He didn't give a hoot about AC or bathrooms with floor-to-ceiling privacy walls.

I don't remember much about the snorkeling itself, just that we did it one day along the Mexican coast on one or the other of the desolate beaches we traveled through that summer. (Were they all desolate, or have I made them so only now?) In my memory, we snorkeled in green water with seaweed and grasses, things I could get caught in, but I am sure my memory is wrong about that, too. Grasses off the Mexican coast? I must have added them for effect all these years later, of what I now see as my tendency back then of getting tangled in things I should not, of not understanding how I might become lost in a certain type of love. Rob was the one who wanted to snorkel, and it was one of the things that I could say yes to without fuss or reservation. I protested hostels. I hated overcrowded and hot buses. I flinched when roaches scurried across tiled floors in motel bathrooms. Rob also wanted to hike some Mexican ruins near Oaxaca, and I said yes, but I must not have told him that, years before, other Mexican ruins had scared me, that once when I had ventured below ground into the dark clay and rock passageways of Teotihuacan, I'd had a panic attack and fled out the way I'd come in and never tried again.

I bought bulky leather hiking boots for that trip to Mexico. The boots were brown and sturdy and tough. And now, nearly two decades after buying them at an outdoor store in Columbus, Ohio, and stuffing them in a green backpack and boarding a plane and trudging onto buses to travel the Mexican coast—which at the start seemed exotic and exciting but three weeks later seemed much less so, to the point where all I wanted was to go home—I still count on those boots for the rockiest of places. They're the only pair I've ever owned. They remind me of all the places I've hiked since then, across snow-capped mountains and grey-stone beaches, through jungled paths and down sliding, treacherous valleys, where I was unsure of my footing but trusted my legs and these ancient boots. And so, I kept on going.

On vacation in the Caribbean, I laced them up for a hike with Preston along the Ram Head Trail, which led to a bald cliff where wind beat against rock, and water bashed stone far below. We stood alone at the peak. When I moved even a little toward the edge, it made Preston nervous, so I stepped back and stayed close. It reminded me of the first time I visited him in Tennessee and had said I wanted to swim in Boone Lake while he was at work. He had asked me to stay close to the shoreline, not to cross the expanse of water alone.

On the return trek, I asked him if he wanted to snorkel in Salt Pond Bay before we made the last trudge to our Jeep. We stripped off our clothes to our swimsuits and left our belongings hanging from a tree branch. We slipped on our fins—mine the hot-pink, his a royal blue.

The water was clear (no seaweed, no grasses). We dove in together, and then we breathed below.

About the Author

Shuly Cawood has an MFA from Queens University, and her creative writing has been published in *Zone 3*, *Prime Number Magazine*, *Rust + Moth*, *Two Cities Review*, and *San Pedro River Review*, among others.

Originally from Ohio, she now lives in Tennessee.

Acknowledgements & Thanks

Whenever my father used to call and ask what I was doing, and I would answer that I was writing, he would pretend to recite the words I had written: "Oh, the father that I have! Such greatness!" or some version of that, and we would both chuckle. But the truth is I would not be a writer without my father—he was and always will be the greatest writer in my life and one of the best people I know. His parenting skills aren't too shabby, either. I want to thank him, my dear mother, and my beautiful sister—Hap, Sonia, Romy.

They taught me loyalty and unfailing love.

Also, many thanks to:

Natalie Kusz and Kathryn Rhett, both of whom advised me on how to strengthen the manuscript, and my Antioch Writers' Workshop posse, especially Melissa Fast, Leslie Pearce-Keating, and Heide Aungst Manfredi, who critiqued parts of this manuscript and made our summer weeks together ones I cherish.

Joyce Dyer, who told me to look for what I had not said in the pages, and then say it.

Matthew Goodman, who told me to refuse to leave the party. I have been doing that ever since, even when I am tired and ready to go home.

My Queenies, who made the MFA an adventure and a gift.

My ex-husband, who read the manuscript without complaint and showed immense grace and kindness.

Tsafi Shalev, who used to ask me to read my writing to her and who had endless faith in my work.

Corinne Mahoney, for being my writing partner and editor extraordinaire.

Emily Fine, for being a tireless reader and friend, and for saying yes, you can.

Jenny Robb, for taking the journey with me, even when it wasn't pretty.

Platypus Press, for caring for my book, for the gentle edits, and for being a publisher I knew instantly was going to fit just right.

Preston McKee, last but never least, for saying everything is going to be okay and making it so, for stirring the oatmeal with me, for being the one.

::

Several parts of this manuscript have been published previously, some in different versions or with different titles. "Young Love," for example, although a true retelling, was originally published as a short story in *Fiction Southeast*. The only revisions were the names of the 'characters' and the point of view of the text (both reverted herein). I gratefully acknowledge the following publications, and their editors, for giving my writing a home:

      "Young Love" in *Fiction Southeast*
      "The Stray" in *Ray's Road Review*

Cont.

"Brave" in *Under the Sun*
        — formed part of "The Compromise"
"The Last Kiss" in *The Louisville Review*
"The Curious Thing about Doubt and Faith"
        in *Full Grown People*
"The Dance" in *Red Earth Review*
"An Unexpected Light" in *Mud Season Review*
"How You Know" in *Rathalla Review*
"A Case, Diagnosis, and Its Findings" in *The Rumpus*
        — formed part of "Luck"

Also Available

Check the Platypus Press website for further releases.

platypuspress.co.uk

CPSIA information can be obtained
at www.ICGtesting.com
Printed in the USA
LVHW03s1528090818
586493LV00001B/196/P